FROM SLAVERY
TO PUBLIC SERVICE

ROBERT SMALLS
1839-1915

Robert Smalls during his years in Congress.

FROM SLAVERY
TO PUBLIC SERVICE
ROBERT SMALLS
1839-1915

OKON EDET UYA

NEW YORK
OXFORD UNIVERSITY PRESS
London 1971 *Toronto*

To My Parents and Grandparents

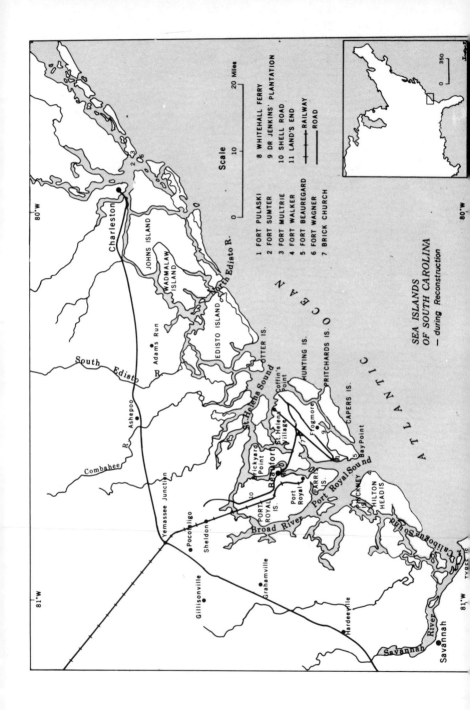

SEA ISLANDS
OF SOUTH CAROLINA
— during Reconstruction

Scale

0   10   20 Miles

1 FORT PULASKI
2 FORT SUMTER
3 FORT MULTRIE
4 FORT WALKER
5 FORT BEAUREGARD
6 FORT WAGNER
7 BRICK CHURCH
8 WHITEHALL FERRY
9 DR JENKINS' PLANTATION
10 SHELL ROAD
11 LAND'S END

••••••••• RAILWAY
———————— ROAD

Charleston

JOHNS ISLAND

WADMALAW ISLAND

EDISTO ISLAND

North Edisto R.

South Edisto

Adams Run

Ashepoo R.

Combahee R.

South

R.

Yemassee Junction

Pocotaligo

Sheldon

Gillisonville

Grahamville

Hardeeville

Savannah

Savannah River

OTTER IS.

Coffin's Point

St. Helena Village

Frogmore

HUNTING IS.

PRITCHARDS IS.

CAPERS IS.

St. Helena Sound

Brickyard Point

Beaufort

PORT ROYAL IS.

Port Royal

Broad River

GARRIS

HILTON HEAD IS.

PINCKNEY

Bay Point

Port Royal Sound

Calibogue Sound

TYBEE IS.

ATLANTIC OCEAN

81°W

80°W

81°W

80°W

0   350

PREFACE

> My race needs no special defense, for the past history of
> them in this country proves them to be the equal of any
> people anywhere. All they need is an equal chance in the
> battle of life.
>
> Robert Smalls
> November 1, 1895

"History often plays strange tricks with reputations," Charles
Cowley wrote in 1882, commenting on the absence of Robert
Smalls' heroic exploits in the then extant histories of the Civil
War. Though Cowley expressed a belief that "a century hence
. . . the hero of the Planter will occupy a much larger place upon
the historian's pages than many others who are now far more
conspicuous," and another contemporary saw Smalls' exploits as
a fit subject for a historical novel, Robert Smalls (1839-1915) has
remained largely neglected by historians.[1] Apart from Dorothy
Sterling's *Captain of the Planter,* written for youthful readers,
there is no adequate biography of this remarkable black politician, despite his wide acclaim as the "most colorful figure in
Republican politics in South Carolina" during the Reconstruc-

[1] Charles Cowley, *The Romance of History in the Black Country and the
Romance of War in the Career of General Robert Smalls* (Lowell, Mass.,
1882); *The Liberator,* May 24, 1865.

vii

tion Era. When he is mentioned in other works, hostile critics dismiss him as one of the "corrupt and irresponsible" Negro politicians who presided over the affairs of "The Prostrate State" of South Carolina during "The Tragic Era" of Reconstruction. More friendly critics crowd him in as just one of the leaders of his community at this difficult time of transition from slavery to freedom. Either treatment is inadequate, and it is hoped that this study will fill the gap.

This book is conceived, in part, as a case study for examining the validity of some historical generalizations about Black Reconstruction and its leaders. How widespread, for example, were the corruption, dishonesty, vindictiveness, incapability and extravagance often attributed to black leaders of this period? Was the movement to overthrow the Reconstruction governments motivated by a strict concern for honesty or political vendetta based on racism? What were the fears, aspirations, hopes, and frustrations of this generation of black Americans? While the life of Smalls alone cannot be used to provide final answers to these questions, this study does suggest that many of the accepted notions about Black Reconstruction cannot stand the test of careful scrutiny. Smalls' active career, stretching from the Civil War to Woodrow Wilson's election, typifies, in many ways, the aspirations and hopes of many blacks during the Civil War and Reconstruction and the tragic betrayal of those hopes in the last decades of the nineteenth and early years of the twentieth centuries.

This book is basically a revision of my doctoral dissertation, "From Servitude to Service: Robert Smalls, 1839-1915," completed at the University of Wisconsin, Madison, in 1969. In both its original and present forms the study profited from contributions from various sources. Professors Elbert B. Smith and Robert Starobin very enthusiastically supervised my work at the University of Wisconsin and gave more than is normally expected of a teacher from a student. Mrs. Dorothy Sterling of Rye, New York, allowed me free access to her rich collection of Robert Smalls material. Mrs. Wright, Principal of Robert Smalls Junior High School, Beaufort, South Carolina, took off time from a busy schedule and at very short notice took me around the Sea

Islands during my short stay in Beaufort. Robert Smalls' descendants, especially Mrs. Elizabeth Hall of Washington, D.C., welcomed me to their homes and frankly discussed the private life of their "Grandpa" with me. Mrs. Helen Christensen of Beaufort shared with me her rich memories of Reconstruction days in the Sea Islands. Professor Hollis Lynch, the general editor of the series, Black Biographies, and Miss Joyce Berry of Oxford University Press, made very useful and critical comments which definitely improved the final form of the manuscript. Other kinds of encouragement throughout the period of study came from my able teachers at the University of Ibadan, Nigeria, Professor J. F. A. Ajayi and Dr. T. N. Tamuno, and Professor Robert July of Hunter College, New York, who introduced me to the study of American History. Professor J. Rogers Hollingsworth and David Cronon of the University of Wisconsin, Madison, were constant sources of encouragement.

Financial support for my studies and subsequent research for this book came from various sources. The Federal Government of Nigeria provided a scholarship for my undergraduate studies. A fellowship from the University of Ibadan, Nigeria, enabled me to come to the United States for graduate work. Funds provided by the Ford Foundation through the Graduate School of the University of Wisconsin at a critical moment in my academic career enabled me to complete my study at Wisconsin, and a Round Table Fellowship made possible research for the final stage of this study. To all these, I am deeply grateful.

Finally, I wish to thank my wife, Bisi, without whose understanding, patience, and encouragement, this book could not have been possible. She typed the many drafts of the manuscript which, in its final form, was carefully put together by Marjorie Pettit of the History Department of the University of Wisconsin.

OKON E. UYA
University of Wisconsin
Madison, Wisconsin
January 1970

CONTENTS

FROM SLAVERY
TO PUBLIC SERVICE

ROBERT SMALLS
1839-1915

I

JUST ANOTHER SLAVE BOY

On May 13, 1862, Captain F. J. Nickols of the *Onward*, the inside ship of the Union fleet blockading Charleston, South Carolina, saw a craft coming out of the heavily fortified port. He ordered his ship swung around so as to train the maximum gunfire on the enemy vessel. Suddenly, he caught sight of a white flag of surrender and ordered his gunners to relax. Unmolested, the Confederate ship drew alongside the *Onward*. Sixteen raggedly dressed blacks (eight men, five women, and three children) emerged and boarded the Union ship. The senior commanding officer of the blockading squadron ordered the fugitives to proceed with their vessel and report to Flag Officer S. F. DuPont. The next morning, the leader of the refugees was ushered aboard the flagship *Wabash* and told his story to the elderly admiral.

This leader was Robert Smalls,[1] heretofore a slave of Henry McKee of Beaufort, South Carolina. Nothing historically accurate is known about Smalls' father, though some say he was a "very distinguished Jew," identified by one contemporary as Moses Goldsmith, a wealthy Charleston merchant. There is also a considerable body of opinion especially among Smalls' descendants,

[1] During slavery and throughout the Civil War, he was known as Robert Small, perhaps because of his stature. In the convention of 1868, however, he was officially enrolled as Robert Smalls. Elizabeth Pearson, ed., *Letters from Port Royal* (Boston, 1906), 268.

that "Grandpa was a product of an illicit affair between Lydia and her master."[2]

Slave children, however, derived their status from that of their mothers. "That the father of a slave is unknown to our law" was the universal understanding of Southern jurists, an official Southern source declared. As one historian put it: "Had status been defined according to the father's condition, there would instantly have arisen the irksome question of what to do with the mulatto children born every year of white planter fathers and slave mothers."[3] Thus, Robert Smalls was known only as the son of his mother, Lydia.

Lydia was born a slave on the Ashdale Plantation, one of John McKee's rice fields located on Ladies Island, about a half hour's row across the river from Beaufort and five hours' sail from Hilton Head at the entrance to Port Royal on the Sea Islands of South Carolina. Apparently born sometime in 1790, Lydia spent her childhood years as a quarter-hand on the plantation, and, though because of her age she escaped the worst features of plantation slavery, she nevertheless experienced material deprivation and overwork that were so much part of the system. As she matured into a girl, she was taken off the plantation and, probably because of her amiability and strong character, made a trusted house servant in John McKee's home on Prince Street, Beaufort. Her daily chores consisted mainly of caring for McKee's five children (Henrietta, Edward, Marguerite, Carolina, and Henry), keeping the house clean, and helping to prepare the meals. As a house servant, Lydia ate good food and wore clothes fashioned after her mistress's own. For much of her mature life, therefore, slavery, for Lydia, involved a minimum of brutality, much "kindness," but little freedom. A woman of courage, per-

[2] Thomas E. Miller, Address of Thomas Miller, February 10, 1930, in Washington, D.C. on the Occasion of Doing Honor to Congressman Oscar DePriest and Three Former Negro Members of Congress Then Living, in Carter G. Woodson Papers, Library of Congress, Washington, D.C., 1. Cowley, The Romance of History, 10. Members of Smalls' family, including Mrs. Elizabeth Hall, Washington, D.C., were interviewed by the writer in January 1969.

[3] Stanley Elkins, Slavery: A Problem in American Life (New York, 1963), 55; H. T. C. Catterall, Judicial Cases Concerning American Slavery and the Negro (2 vols., Washington, D.C., 1926), I, 287.

sistency, intellect and spiritual hope, Lydia, however, never allowed herself to be lulled by the kindness of John McKee and his family into a false sense of what slavery really meant. As late as 1955, Smalls' son, William, still remembered, however vaguely, the many family stories of Lydia's strictness, strong character, and desire to terminate her servitude.[4]

Lydia's son, Robert, was born on April 5, 1839, in the McKee slave quarters on Prince Street. He grew up in this household, and, apparently because of his intelligence and kind disposition, possibly because of his mother's "affair" with the master, he very early won the liking of John McKee and, with that, much freedom of behavior in the household. John's son, Henry McKee, born when Lydia was twenty-one, and nursed by Lydia herself, inherited Robert and Lydia, together with a substantial amount of property, on his father's death in 1848; Robert was his favorite servant, and, as such, tended his master's horse, rowed the boat when he went fishing, and carried the bow when he went hunting. Prior to 1851 when he was hired out, therefore, Robert, a notch above other slaves, grew up in relative comfort. John McKee's nephew, W. B. McKee, later recalled the kind treatment Robert received as a child, and a granddaughter of Henry McKee's remembered that she "never heard my parents speak of him [Smalls] except in a kindly way."[5]

Despite these happy surroundings, the future did not appear propitious for the slave boy. "He never forgot," wrote one of his contemporaries, "being a slave that his elevated position could be changed in a night and the most brutal servitude inflicted upon him, because he was not even master of his own soul . . . there was so much uncertainty with his being that the dread of changed conditions became a nightmare that tortured him by

[4] William Smalls to Dorothy Sterling, 1955, in Dorothy Sterling's Collection of Robert Smalls' Material, Rye, New York; Dorothy Sterling, *Captain of the Planter* (New York, 1958), 25-36; Willie Lee Rose, *Rehearsal for Reconstruction: The Port Experiment* (New York, 1964), 131; J. Irving Washington, Sr., "General Robert Smalls," *Colored American Magazine* (1904).

[5] Mabel Runnette of Beaufort to Dorothy Sterling, April 9, 1956; W. B. McKee to Wade Hampton, n.d., Hampton Papers, Box 14, Folder 14, South Carolina Archives, Columbia, South Carolina. See also, S. D. Smith, *The Negro in Congress, 1870-1901* (Chapel Hill, N.C., 1940), 67.

night and haunted him by day." Maternal care also intensified Robert Smalls' anxiety about the future. Later accounts suggest that, when he was growing up as a pampered pet in the Prince Street house of John McKee, Lydia was afraid her son did not realize the meaning of slavery. To prevent him from being taken in by the comfort in which he lived, Lydia forced Robert to watch slaves being whipped in the yard of a Beaufort jail and often took him around the arsenal where slaves were auctioned. She also told him stories about the sufferings of slaves and tried to instill a spirit of identification between him and his less fortunate fellows by constantly teasing him with orders to "Go out there in the yard where you belong." In these various ways young Robert was made to realize the difference between the appearances of his life and the harsh realities of being a slave.

What Robert failed to learn about the indignities of slavery from his mother, Beaufort was well equipped to supply. A pleasant little town on Port Royal, an island in the archipelago off the coast of South Carolina and Georgia known as the Sea Islands, Beaufort, founded by the Spaniards in the sixteenth century but settled by the English toward the end of the seventeenth, had, by the time of the Civil War, become the only town in the whole region above the size of a village. Serving as a resort area for planters in the neighboring region, the town had an unstable population which varied from two thousand in winter to four thousand in summer when the rich planters came in. A constant and very conspicuous element in the population was provided by black people. They had been brought here since colonial times to work the rich cotton and rice fields for which the area was famous. A prominent sector of the early white settlers had come from Barbados, and they had brought with them the discriminatory attitudes and customs toward slaves which had developed in the West Indies. Soon, large property holdings in staple crops and black slaves became the characteristic economic features of the islands. By 1861, the black laboring force, living and working under a very strict slave code, constituted 82.8 per cent of the entire Beaufort population. Apart from the house servants, the so-called Negro aristocracy, most of these blacks lived a miserable existence on the plantations. Their broad backs and nimble fingers made possible the prosperity of the town, but the black slaves shared little of it. In contrast to their poor houses stood the handsome mansions of the rich planters, which, flanked by magnolia and orange trees and furnished with mahogany and rosewood, attested to the wealth of their owners. This prosperity of the planters in the midst of the misery of the slaves was a painful reminder to slave boys like Robert who soon learned that the blacks toiled for the enjoyment of others. Moreover, there was a constant display of the power of the planters calculated to frighten would-be slave rebels into submission. In later life Robert recalled being frightened by the constant artillery displays in Beaufort. Such a situation was, in fact, one that called for constant self-questioning and examination.[6]

The latitude for such examination was broadened for Robert when he was brought by his master to Charleston. In 1851 Henry McKee sold out his real estate at Beaufort to the De Treville family, bought a plantation called "Cobcall" near Charleston, and moved there.[7] Smalls was hired out to Charleston where he lived till the Civil War.

Charleston, the great cosmopolitan cultural center of the Old South, was described by one contemporary at this time as "rich, powerful, aristocratic and dictatorial." It was well calculated to bring both hope and despair to an intelligent and ambitious slave. The rich planters often congregated there to discuss the thorny problems of the 1850's. The free Negro community was also strong in Charleston; there were black masons, carpenters, glaziers, blacksmiths, barbers, cooks, painters, and pilots, most

[6] A. W. Stephens, ed., *Enfranchisement and Citizenship: Addresses and Papers by E. L. Pearson* (Boston, 1896), 69; Pearson, *Letters from Port Royal*, 8. William Smalls to Dorothy Sterling, 1955; Mabel Runnette to Dorothy Sterling, April 9, 1956.

[7] Mrs. Mann, Henry McKee's grandaughter, maintains that her grandparents did not move to Charleston until the time of the Federal occupation. All other sources indicate that the family actually moved to Charleston in 1851. The plantation name "Cobcall" appears to be a misprint for "Hobcaw," a plantation near Georgetown. See Mabel Runnette to Dorothy Sterling, April 9, 1956; William Smalls, "Robert Smalls," Schomburg Collection; Washington, "General Robert Smalls"; Benjamin Quarles, "Abduction of the 'Planter,'" *Civil War History*, IV (March 1958), 7; Carter G. Woodson, "Robert Smalls and his Descendants," *Negro History Bulletin* (November 1947).

of whom had worked and saved enough money to buy their freedom. In 1850, free Negroes worked at fifty-six different occupa-
tions in the city, and, in 1859, four hundred of them paid taxes
on property assessed at $724,570. Although these Charleston
blacks had developed into "a respectable, economically independent and class-conscious group," they did not escape the
stigma of slavery since whites regarded a free Negro as a dangerous example to the bondsmen. They were thus required to wear
identifying tags around their necks and have white men act
as their guardians.[8]

In Charleston, Robert was first hired as a waiter at the Planter's
Hotel where he worked for six months. Here he attended not
only foreign visitors, but also the rich planters and their families
who came there for the social season. On several occasions he
overheard the aristocrats of the South discussing the prospects of
extending slavery—the very system his mother had taught him
to regard as the source of his indignity. Smalls next got a job
with the city contractor as a lamplighter and held the position
for eight months. With a rag slung over his shoulder and a ladder
hooked under his arm, he traveled from street corner to corner
wiping out the lamp globes and cleaning the soot from the jets.
He repeated the rounds in the afternoon, this time armed with a
long taper with which to light the lamps.

Robert seems to have gradually grown restless and longed for a
freer life, for which the waterfront of Charleston provided him
with an opportunity. His love for swimming also drew him to
the waterfront. He became first a stevedore in Charleston harbor
and later a foreman. He was then employed by John Simmons, a
Charleston rigger, to drive hoisting horses on the wharf for one
year. Impressed by the boy's "energy, push and stickability,"
Simmons put him to work in his rigging loft in the winter where
he learned the trade of sailmaker and rigger. In the summers he
worked on a coasting schooner as a sailor. Soon, he began to
handle boats with such skill and assurance that Simmons once

[8] Horace E. Ritchett, "The Traditions of the Free Negro in Charleston,
South Carolina," *Journal of Negro History* (April 1940), 139; Roi Ottley,
Black Odyssey: The Story of the Negro in America (New York, 1949), 98.

remarked to one of his customers: "That boy's got the makings of a pilot. Ever see him at the bar when the tide's going out? 'Stead of dropping anchor and waiting for high tide he just backs up the ship and rides in with the swell."[9]

According to law, Robert's earnings up to this time had to be turned over to his master. Anxious for greater freedom and more control over his own life, he offered to make his own arrangements to hire himself out, and agreed to pay his master fifteen dollars a month. These terms were accepted by Henry McKee, and from 1857 Robert became his own master as far as employment was concerned.

Shortly before this occurred, Smalls was married to Hannah Jones, a slave of Samuel Kingman, and also offered to purchase her time at seven dollars a month. Their first daughter, Elizabeth Lydia Small, was born on February 12, 1858. By law both Elizabeth and Hannah were slaves of Samuel Kingman. Apparently disturbed by the status of his daughter and wife, Robert decided to buy their freedom. Kingman was struck by "the frank manhood" displayed by the slave father and agreed to sell Robert's wife and daughter for eight hundred dollars. By 1861 Robert had apparently saved up to seven hundred dollars for the purchase money. The war, however, gave him the opportunity to take his family with him on his flight to freedom, and the money was never paid. But contemporaries described Smalls' intent to purchase the freedom of his family as "noble" and contended that the fact that the money was not actually paid "did not rob [the] action of its nobility."[10]

The next few months were very busy ones for Robert Smalls. He pored over maps and charts, traced channels, studied currents and tides, and memorized the location of the shoals and reefs in Charleston harbor to better equip himself for the challenges of making money from the waterfront. By the time of the Civil War Smalls had complete mastery of the harbors and waterways of the South Carolina and Georgia seacoasts. He became an expert seaman and a great manager of boats; few men along the south

[9] Cited by Sterling, *Captain of the Planter*, 45.

[10] Washington, "General Robert Smalls," 2.

Atlantic coast had better knowledge of the shoals and deep currents than Smalls.

The years immediately preceding the Civil War brought great
anxiety to the Sea Island blacks. On the national scene, the com-
promises of the 1850's had failed to settle the slavery controversy.
The indifference displayed by many Northern states over the
enforcement of the fugitive slave laws, the increasing denunciation of the "peculiar institution" of the South in the Northern
press, the suspected insincerity by the South of Northern intentions over the issue of slavery, and the attempt by the South to
re-open the African slave trade in defiance of Northern public
opinion, combined to deal a blow to the spirit of these compro-
mises. The South feared slave revolts incited by the abolitionists,
and the raid of John Brown at Harper's Ferry in 1859 only
heightened the tension. South Carolina, which had been in a
state of constant excitement since the attempted Denmark Vesey
slave revolt in Charleston in 1822, responded to these threats by
tightening its slave laws. Owners no longer allowed their slaves
to travel from one plantation to another or to visit the cities on
Sundays. The patrols were intensified and fewer passes were
issued. It was rumored that the state legislature was considering
laws to confiscate the property of free blacks and even to return
them to slavery.[11]

It is difficult to recapture the exact feelings of Sea Island blacks
when the firing on Fort Sumter began. Undoubtedly, in the confusion that followed, many were torn between fidelity to their
masters and the desire for freedom. Some maintained that they
did not know where to go, because they had always depended on
their masters to look after them. Mary Boykin Chesnut, wife of
a South Carolina senator, recorded in her diary on April 13, 1861,
that, though Fort Sumter had been on fire, "not by one word or
look can we detect any change in the demeanor of these Negro

[11] For a brief discussion of the situation and the breakdown of the com-
promises in the 1850's, see the following: George W. Williams, *History of the
Negro Race in America, 1619-1880* (2 vols. 1883); John Hope Franklin, *From
Slavery to Freedom* (Chicago, London, 1947); Elbert B. Smith, *The Death of
Slavery* (Chicago, 1967), 94-142. For the situation in South Carolina see John
Lofton, *Insurrection in South Carolina: The Turbulent World of Denmark
Vesey* (Yellow Springs, Ohio, 1964).

servants. Lawrence sits at our door, as sleepy and as respectful, as profoundly indifferent. So are they all. . . . You could not tell they even hear the awful noise that is going on in the bay, though it is dinning in their ears night and day." After the capture of Port Royal in 1861, some blacks reproached the Northern missionaries who came there and insisted that there was no confusion when they belonged to their masters. Some apparently were not prepared to exchange the certain protection of slavery for the rosy but seemingly unrealizable promises of freedom.[12]

There is considerable reason to believe, however, that many blacks in the Sea Islands behaved in a way to justify the thesis that "from the day of the firing on Fort Sumter, Negroes had envisioned the situation as an irrepressible moral conflict between slavery and liberty, and a war for the rights of man in fulfillment of the genius of the American democratic faith." Even among her seemingly indifferent servants, Mrs. Chesnut noted that Dick, the butler, "won't look at me now. He looks over my head. He scents freedom in the air." When slave child Sam Mitchell was confused by the roar of guns over the Sea Islands, he was calmed down by his mother's assurance that the roar was not thunder, but the Yankee guns come to bring freedom. Asked which he liked better, slavery or freedom, a black slave is reported to have replied that in slavery he owned nothing and never would have while in freedom he owned the home and raised the family, with all the worry of both, and in slavery he had no worries—but that he chose freedom. To a similar question another replied that while he was a slave he did not have any responsibility, did not have to worry about something to eat and wear and a place to sleep . . . but that did not make up for not being free.[13] Charlotte Forten, a Yankee teacher and herself a mulatto, later remembered how the Sea Islanders never wearied of telling their Northern teachers how panic-stricken and fright-

[12] Cited in B. A. Botkin, *Lay My Burden Down* (Chicago, 1945), 236-237; Ben Ames Williams, ed., *A Diary from Dixie* (Boston, 1949), 38; Pearson, *Letters from Port Royal*, 15.
[13] August Meier, "Negroes in the First and Second Reconstruction," *Civil War History* (August 1967), 116; Williams, *A Diary*, 293; Slave Narrative Collection (WPA Federal Writers Project), XIV, III, 203; Botkin, *Lay My Burden Down*, 267.

ened their masters were when the war began. Asked why he did not flee with his master, Harry, a plantation foreman, explained that, although his master tried to persuade him that the Yankees would either shoot black slaves who remained behind or sell them into slavery in Cuba, he stayed because he reasoned that there was no difference between slavery in Cuba or for the Yankees and what he had gone through already. Actually, Harry had been informed by a black leader that the Yankees were their friends and they would be free when the Yankees came. Colonel Thomas Higginson, first commander of black troops during the Civil War, reported an old former slave's account of how some slaves, urged by their masters to run to the wood to hide from the Yankees, actually ran in the opposite direction toward the boats bringing in the Yankees. With most of the Port Royal area masters fled to Charleston, many of the coastal blacks held secret meetings and pledged to strike for their freedom as soon as they saw a chance of success.[14]

Robert Smalls was in Charleston where Southern enthusiasm ran high over the capture of Fort Sumter. From the type of information he later gave to the Federal forces that attacked the city, it is conceivable that he attended several of the secret black meetings held in that city. He remembered later that "we heard the words of hope amid the din of battle and the clash of arms. We began to realize that we were human beings." In Charleston, he had observed and shared the miserable position of his people, and he also acquired a business acumen and a sense of service. "He was educated practically in the school of contact with the very best cultured minds of business men on the wharves and warehouses in the city of Charleston," Thomas Miller would later remember, "a kind of education that fits a man for service." Robert Smalls was indeed very soon to render his first public service—a blow for freedom with the abduction of the cotton steamer, the *Planter*.[15]

[14] Charlotte Forten, "Life on the Sea Islands," *Atlantic Monthly* (May 1864), 393; Thomas Higginson, "Up the Edisto," *Atlantic Monthly* (August 1867), 161.

[15] *Congressional Record*, 49th Congress, 1st Session, 1885, Appendix, 391-320; Miller, "Address," 3.

II

A CIVIL WAR BLACK HERO

ROBERT SMALLS' abduction of the *Planter* has until recently been the only event saving him from total oblivion in historical writing. Though actually less important than his subsequent political career, this spectacular deed was the turning point in Smalls' life. Requiring careful planning and brilliant execution, the deed revealed the courage, audacity, and love of freedom that would endear Smalls to his people and assure his political ascendancy in the years after the war.[1]

Built in Charleston, South Carolina, in 1860, the *Planter* was a cotton steamer plying the Pee Dee River. It was 150 feet long and 7 feet 10 inches deep, had a ten-foot beam, and could carry 1,400 bales of cotton.[2] During the summer of 1861, Smalls was em-

[1] Studies dealing with Smalls' abduction of the ship include the following: Quarles, "Abduction of the 'Planter' "; M. Rosbow, "The Abduction of the Planter," *Crisis* (April 1949); J. W. Simmons, "Hon. Robert Smalls," in *Men of the Mark* (Ohio, 1887). Sterling's *Captain of the Planter* is a romanticized but thoroughly researched version for younger readers. Congressional action on the issue can be found in "Bill Authorizing the President to Place Robert Smalls on the Retired List of the Navy," *House Report*, 47th Congress, 2nd Session, 1883. Important statements by army officers including DuPont and Parrot are reprinted. Hereafter cited as *Report 1887*.

[2] Quarles, Abduction of the 'Planter,' " 5-6 gives these measurements. The Old Army Section reported that the ship was 156 feet long, 46 feet wide, and 7 feet deep at the time of capture. A New York document gives the ship's measurements as 159 feet 8 inches by 35 feet 4 inches by 6 feet 8 inches, Records of Smalls and the *Planter*, National Archives, Washington; Also Morris Reiger to Dorothy Sterling, December 4, 1956.

ployed as a sailor on the ship by owner John Ferguson for a
meager salary of sixteen dollars a month, fifteen of which he
turned over to Henry McKee. He supplemented his remaining
dollar by engaging in petty trading while aboard the ship.

Late in 1861, the Confederate government chartered the
Planter and converted it into a special dispatch boat for General
Roswell Ripley, second-in-command of Charleston's defenses. The
carrying capacity of the ship, calculated at a thousand men, made
her particularly suitable for this enterprise. She was armed with
one long thirty-two-pound pivot gun on the foredeck and a
twenty-four-pound Howitzer file on the afterdeck. From time to
time the ship was also used in the engineering department to
help in the construction of new fortifications on the Middle
Ground in Charleston harbor and in carrying supplies to other
fortifications in the neighboring waters.

Being a slave, Smalls was forced to remain on the vessel when
the Confederates acquired it. Soon, he "demonstrated to the
officers his abilities and perfect knowledge of the harbor inlets
around Charleston," and was consequently elevated to the position of wheelman. This was a position of trust and honor. Actually, Smalls was the pilot of the ship but was called a wheelman
because it was not in accordance with Confederate nautical eti-
quette to call a black man pilot! Often, Smalls sailed the *Planter*
down the coast making a survey of Confederate forts. He helped
destroy Federal lighthouses on Hunting Island and to lay torpedoes in the Edisto and Stono rivers. He carried carpenters and
masons, lumber, cannons, and soldiers for the construction of
new Confederate forts at Bay Point and Hilton Head, Fort Beauregard and Fort Walker. From a safe anchorage in the Beaufort
River, Smalls watched the Union fleet, led by the U. S. S. *Wabash,*
attack and bring under Union control the Port Royal area, including his native Beaufort, in November of 1861. From refugees
who fled from the area to Charleston, he heard about complete
devastation of Beaufort and, perhaps more important, learned
that his mother had refused to flee and had been left. By the end
of 1861, Smalls had learned the signals necessary to pass Confederate forts and batteries in the harbor as well as the location
of the hidden mines.

The months following the capture of Port Royal were anxious ones for Robert. Looking through the ship captain's field glasses from Charleston, he could see the Union fleet anchored just beyond the bar. He heard through the grapevine that the blacks who remained behind after the capture of Port Royal were no longer slaves, and, though not technically free since they were treated as "contraband" war property subject to seizure by the Union forces, they were being helped along by the Union army. His mother had sent a message indicating that she was well and happy, living in her old room and cooking for the Union soldiers. He constantly brooded over the differences between his slavery and his mother's "freedom," always realizing that but a few miles separated him from his mother's lot.

One day, one of Smalls' black companions on the *Planter* began to joke about abducting the ship. Smalls immediately took up the hint and cautioned the crew against alluding to the matter. He told them, however, that, if they wanted to discuss it seriously, they should meet in his house to devise a plan "to place themselves under the protection of the Stars and Stripes instead of the Stars and Bars." Accordingly they met, proposed various plans, but finally left the arrangement for the escape to the discretion of Smalls, his companions promising to obey him and be ready to accompany him at a moment's notice. Meanwhile, Smalls brooded over the matter for three days and put his family and those of his fellow planners on constant alert.

On a Sunday afternoon in April, the black crew of the *Planter* gathered in Smalls' room on East Bay Street to listen to the plan. The women and children would be hidden on a merchant ship in the Cooper River. Under cover of darkness, they would be picked up in the *Planter,* and the party would then head for the Union blockading fleet beyond the bar. It was a simple plan fraught with great dangers, and success would depend on how opportune the moment of execution would be.

Smalls continued as pilot aboard the *Planter* until May 12, 1862, when he was presented with a chance to make his move. Apparently believing in the docility of the slaves or trusting in their fidelity, the white crew of the ship, including the captain, chief engineer, and mate, had all gone into town leaving on board a crew of eight blacks, among them Robert Smalls. The previous night two hundred pounds of ammunition and four guns had been loaded on the ship for transport to the harbor battery. Believing that this cargo could be of considerable use to "Uncle Abe," Smalls had deliberately slowed down the loading of the ship in order to prevent its planned departure to the battery.

As soon as the white crew had left, Smalls alerted the ship's black crew, including two engineers, John Smalls (no relative) and Alfred Gradine, and six other blacks, Abraham Jackson, Gabriel Turno, William Morrison, Samuel Chisholm, Abraham Allston, and David Jones. The ship steamed up to the North Atlantic Wharf where Smalls' wife and child, together with four other women and one other child, were taken aboard. The venture was hazardous in the extreme. The *Planter* would have to pass beneath the guns of the batteries in the harbor. Detection would mean certain death, but the daring resolution to strike a blow for freedom had been made. Knowing he could expect little mercy if caught, Smalls bound the party to agree to blow up the ship rather than be taken alive if they were unable to make good their flight.

At 3:00 A.M. the great deception began. The hawsers which moored the ship to the Southern Wharf were cast off. The wharf signal was sounded and answered, and so began the perilous journey along the heavily fortified coast. Bristling with sea defenses, the Charleston harbor was ringed with forts and batteries on constant alert. Between the wharf where the *Planter* was moored and the Federal fleet upon the high seas, there were five forts heavily manned with various kinds of cannon. Smalls had been passing one or the other of these fortifications with munitions and provision for one or the other of the garrisons, and knew the appropriate signal for passing each of them.

He hoisted the vessel's two flags, Confederate and Palmetto, and eased into the inner channel. He geared the ship to its customary pace. With coolness and great presence of mind, he looked into the muzzle of the guns and gave the signals. His knowledge of things necessary to be done in such trying hours came into full play. Wearing the captain's hat and mimicking his gait,

Smalls stood in the pilot house with the cord in his hand. Fort Johnson was passed with the steam whistle blowing the usual salute. The ship then proceeded down the bay toward historic Fort Sumter. "Oh, Lord," Smalls prayed, according to one source, "we entrust ourselves into thy hands. Like thou didst for the Israelites in Egypt, please stand guard over us and guide us to our promised land of freedom."[3] Carefully giving the appropriate signal, two long whistles and a short, Smalls cut through the inland waterway into the open sea. The pace was doubled, and soon the escaped slaves encountered a Federal blockading fleet of ten warships off Otter Island. The *Planter's* crew lowered their guns, ran up a bed sheet as a flag of surrender, and gave three cheers for the Union. Captain Nichols of the *Onward* boarded the *Planter,* and received Smalls and his crew. In the evening of the same day Smalls reached Hilton Head and delivered his cargo of Confederate artillery to the Federal authorities.

The news of the abduction of the *Planter* spread rapidly through the country. *Harper's Weekly* published a photograph of Robert Smalls alongside that of the ship, declaring that this was "one of the most daring and heroic adventures since the war commenced." "If we must still remember with humility that the Confederate flag yet waves where our national colors were first struck," wrote the New York *Tribune,* "we should be all more prompt to recognize the merit that has put into our possession the first trophy from Fort Sumter. . . . A slave has brought away under the very guns of the enemy, where no fleet of ours has yet dared to venture, a prize whose possession a commodore thinks worthy to be announced in a special dispatch." The Count of Paris, reporting the Civil War for French audiences, wrote of "the remarkable incident" and the "daring and intelligent Negro" who carried it out.[4]

The incident was of great importance to the fortunes of the contending parties in the Port Royal theater of war. The loss of the ship by the Confederates at a time when they were desper-

---

[3] Rosbow, "The Abduction of the Planter," 106.

[4] *Harper's Weekly,* June 14, 1862, 372. New York *Tribune* cited by William W. Brown, *The Black man: His Antecedents, His Genuis, and His Achievements* (Boston, 1863), 80.

ately looking for outside help was a blow to both morale and military capacity. Voicing the general indignation of Confederate South Carolina over the negligence of the white officers of the ship, the Columbia *Guardian* expressed a fervent wish that "the recreant parties will be brought to speedy justice, and the prompt penalty of the halter rigorously enforced." The community was "intensely agitated on Tuesday morning by the intelligence that the steamer *Planter* had been taken possession of by her colored crew and boldly run out to the blockaders," the Charleston *Daily Courier* wrote. "The news at first was not credited." The *Providence Journal* was equally impressed. "See what has come to pass," the paper editorialized. "A steamer, cannons, ammunition worth $30,000 are furnished to Duepont [sic], nine chattels losing all regard for the curse pronounced against Ham, are set free, and we know not what other Divine arrangements are interfered with." From army headquarters in Richmond came a dispatch to General Pamberton stating that General Lee "very much regrets the circumstances relative to the *Planter*'s escape and hopes that necessary measures will be taken to prevent any repetition of a like misfortune."[5]

The Union's gain was more than symbolic. A month later, Admiral DuPont wrote that he was glad "that the *Planter* had proved so useful a transport, and that we have again been able so materially to aid the army, especially at a critical time, when its generals were almost helpless for want of transports." On May 14, 1862 DuPont also reported that the steamer was "quite an acquisition to the squadron by her good machinery and very light drought." The *Planter*, *Harper's Weekly* maintained, was "just such a vessel as is needed to navigate the shallow waters between Hilton Head and the adjacent islands, and will prove almost invaluable to the government." John Dezendorf, Chairman of a Special Congressional Committee appointed to determine a re-appraisal of the *Planter* in 1883, reported that "the loss of the ship was a severe blow to the enemy's service in carry-

[5] Columbia *Guardian*, May 17, 1862; Charleston *Daily Courier*, May 14, 1862; *Providence Journal* cited by *The National Anti-Slavery Standard*, May 31, 1862.

ing supplies and troops to different points of the harbor and river fortifications."[6]

Overnight, the unknown slave boy was catapulted into national fame and attention, a symbol of the ability of black slaves to fight for their freedom. "The moral effect of such practical emancipation," John Forbes, a Boston businessman with abolitionist sympathies, declared, "was worth much more than money." Hitherto, argued Congressman William Kelley of Pennsylvania, in an address before some Charleston blacks in 1865, "there was nothing at all to show that the Negro could do without a white leader, but there came the *Planter* which Robert Smalls, the black man, had taken by his own command from the armed state of South Carolina, showing that your race have enterprise, energy, capacity, and may be trusted to go alone, at least on steamboats." Smalls was seen by Admiral DuPont to be "superior to any one who have come into our line." He felt that the bringing out of the ship under all the circumstances "would have done credit to any one." One contemporary later argued that "no one but a hero, a natural born hero, would have conceived this idea thru danger and death to freedom." In the conception and execution of "this perilous act," he continued, Smalls became "a hero of the War of the sixties, the equal of any one connected with that war." In October 1865, the black leader, Frederick Douglass, in his inaugural address at Douglass Institute, Baltimore, argued that the "great actions as shown by Robert Smalls and others" should have been sufficient to change the general public estimate of the Negro race.[7]

Robert Smalls' abduction of the *Planter* also featured prominently in the wartime debate over emancipation. "What a painful instance we have here of the Negro's inability to take care of himself," the *Providence Journal* taunted slavery defenders. "If Smalls had a suitable white overseer, he would never have done

[6] *Official Records, Union and Confederate Navies, War of Rebellion,* Series 1, Vol. 12, 807, 820-826; DuPont to Gideon Wales, May 14, 1862, *Report 1887; Harper's Weekly,* June 14, 1862.

[7] John M. Forbes to Charles Sumner, May 16, 1862, *Official Records;* Charleston *Daily Courier,* April 7, 1865; Miller, "Address," 4; Phillip Foner ed., *The Life and Writings of Frederick Douglass* (4 vols., New York, 1950-55), IV, 179.

this foolish and thoughtless thing. Such fellows need a superior who is familiar with the intentions of divine providence and who could tell them where they were meant to stay." Others wondered whether those Northerners who were against emancipation were "also in favor of taking Robert Small [sic] and chucking him back under the cowskin [whip] of the rebel knave who used to work him for nothing." The abolitionist newspaper, *The Liberator,* editorialized that Smalls' heroism was one of the several instances that proved the black man's loyalty to the Union and his right to be free.[8]

Equally impressed by Smalls' show of heroism was Major-General David Hunter, who had superseded General T. W. Sherman as the commander of the Department of the South at Port Royal in mid-March 1862. "Very frank in his abolitionist convictions," and suspected to have been sent to Port Royal as a result of abolitionist pressure on the War Department, Hunter had, two weeks after his arrival, clarified the status of contrabands within his jurisdiction by declaring them free men. Also interpreting an earlier order to organize blacks within his command into "squads, companies, or otherwise" as actual authorization to raise black troops, Hunter had set about doing just that from blacks on the plantations. His action, however, had drawn considerable disapproval from a politically astute and racially conscious administration, and he had been forced to disband his black recruits. Meanwhile, controversy was raging in the nation over the military desirability and capability of black soldiers. Hunter felt that the impression created by the heroic act of Smalls and the presence of the hero himself in Washington might influence the government to reassess its position and come out in behalf of his black wards.

On August 16, 1862, Hunter sent Smalls, accompanied by the Reverend Mansfield French, the Methodist chaplain of the Military Hospital in Hilton Head and a zealot for the "contraband" cause, to Washington to persuade President Lincoln and War Secretary Edwin Stanton to permit the enlistment of Port Royal

8 *National Anti-Slavery Standard,* May 31, 1862, quoting the *Providence Journal,* also June 21, 1862; *The Liberator,* May 12, 1862.

"contrabands" into the Union army. Smalls and French went to Washington and were "honored with several interviews with President Lincoln and Secretary Stanton." They also met with several other members of the cabinet. French, a persuasive speaker, certainly had in Robert Smalls the most dramatic indication of the capacity of blacks to fight, not only for the Union, but also for their freedom. Shortly afterward, he wrote that he had accomplished "all I came for" and that Smalls had regaled Treasury Secretary Salmon Chase "for almost an hour with his thrilling story."[9]

Smalls personally carried back to South Carolina an all-important note in which Secretary Stanton directed General Rufus Saxton, Chief Quartermaster at Port Royal, to organize in squads, companies, battalions, regiments, or brigades "colored persons of African descent . . . and muster them into the service of the United States for the term of the war." The blacks were to be paid at most five dollars compensation a month, fed, clothed and cared for "in the same manner as other persons in the Quartermaster's service." Officers were to be appointed to instruct them in military drill, discipline, and duty. In addition, General Saxton could use "all the islands and plantations heretofore occupied by the government and secure and harvest the crops, and cultivate and improve the plantations." Most important, all black slaves admitted into the service of the government, together with their wives and children, were declared "forever free," and were to be so treated and regarded.[10]

Back in Beaufort, Robert Smalls worked to arouse the interest of the Sea Islanders in the opportunities offered by military service. This was not easy because many a Sea Islander regarded serving in the army as an exchange of private for public servitude. Smalls was not discouraged, however, and stressed with both passion and eloquence not only the economic prospects, but also

---

[9] French to George Whipple, August 23, 1862, cited by Rose, *Rehearsal*, 190; Sterling's account of the interview, *Captain of the Planter*, 103-105, was based essentially on what Frederick Douglass and other black leaders said Lincoln was like.

[10] Secretary Stanton to General Saxton, August 22, 1862, Records, War Department, National Archives.

the challenge of freedom involved in serving the country. Response was generally favorable, and the volunteers were mustered in at Old Fort, South Carolina, about four miles from Beaufort. Known as the First Carolina Volunteers, this regiment was eventually incorporated into the famous Sixth Massachusetts under Thomas Higginson.

Smalls himself could not be enlisted directly into the Federal Navy because standing regulations demanded that enlisted men had to be graduates of a naval school. Instead, he was commissioned as a Second Lieutenant, Company B, 33rd Regiment, United States Colored Troops, and was then detailed to act as pilot abroad the *Planter.* "The accession of Smalls," commented a reporter for the *Philadelphia Inquirer,* "is deemed of more importance than the heavy guns of the *Planter* as Smalls is thoroughly acquainted with all the intricacies of navigation in that region."[11]

As pilot aboard the *Planter* and other Union ships, Smalls made repeated trips on the rivers near the coast pointing out and helping to remove the torpedoes which he himself had assisted in sinking and putting into position. On one occasion, he piloted the *Planter* up the Broad River to Pocotaligo, leading a fleet of gunboats and transports to destroy the railroad bridges on the Charleston-Savannah line. In all, Smalls fought in seventeen battles during the war, and was prominent in several engagements.

Among these engagements was one Union attack on Charleston in 1863. When the Union troops were massed to attack the city, Smalls told them that the fighting force of the Confederates in that area consisted largely of blacks who, though the most exact discipline was enforced among them, would desert in thousands and flock to the Union lines. He asked to be allowed to go with the land forces, boastfully promising that in less than ten days he would have more than ten thousand fully-armed blacks who would be of greater service to the Union war effort than an equal number of white soldiers. When the attack came in April, Smalls did go with the naval forces. He piloted the *Keokuk,* a double-

11 *Philadelphia Inquirer,* May 17, 1862, cited by the *National Republican,* May 20, 1862.

turreted monster commanded by Captain Rhind and used as the
rear-ship for the Union ironclads which went into action against
the city. Led by the *Weehawken,* the Union fleet was caught
unawares by a rain of Confederate cannonballs as they rounded
Morris Island and headed for Charleston. It was difficult to man-
euver the Union monitors in the narrow channel. Soon, the
Weehawken's propeller was fouled in rebel nets; another ship,
the *Ironsides,* veered off her course and got into the way of other
ships behind. As confusion mounted, the Commanding Officer,
Admiral DuPont, signaled to disregard the order of battle, and
it soon became every ship for herself against the enemy. Smalls,
who knew the area thoroughly, and whose ship could navigate
in shallow water much more easily than the monitors, was ordered
by Rhind to steer past the other ships toward Fort Sumter. He
immediately cruised past the monitors, and steamed toward the
fort, only to come under heavy fire from the Confederates. For a
moment the ship drifted aimlessly with the tide. After a few
hours, the *Keokuk* lurched drunkenly and plunged underneath
the waves. "The captain did all a good captain could do to save
the vessel and its crew," historian David Potter later commented
on the incident. "The crew had fought two great battles in a
short time, one with the Confederates, and the other with the
wrath of the ocean, and in both cases they had shown that in-
domitable courage and skill which are among the highest attri-
butes of American sailors." Robert Smalls, the pilot of the ship,
had the honor of belonging to the little band of courageous
survivors. "The boat was struck ninety-six times," he later boasted
to his son, and "the wheelman beside me was struck flush in the
face."[12]

On May 20, 1863, Smalls also led three Union gunboats across
the bar that marked the entrance of the Stono River and directed the gunboats in their attack on Stono. The commanding
officer of the expedition, E. G. Parrot, credited the successful completion of their mission to "information derived mainly from the
contraband pilot Smalls."[13]

[12] David D. Potter, *The Naval History of the Civil War* (New York, 1960),
414; William Smalls to Dorothy Sterling, August 24, 1955.
[13] *The Liberator,* March 27, 1863; also *Report 1887.*

Smalls displayed great courage in an incident involving the
Planter on one of her trips through the mouth of the Stono
River, near Folly Creek. While the ship was passing through the
inlet, the Confederates attempted to hem her in and recapture
her by placing three batteries along the Kiawah River. Because
the batteries were on a high bluff, it was almost impossible for
the shells to strike the *Planter* below the water line, but the
smoke stack, the lookout tower, and the roof of the wheel house
in which Smalls sat were hit. Believing there was little chance
of escape, the *Planter's* captain ordered Smalls to beach the ship
and surrender. "Not by a damned sight will I beach this boat
for you," Smalls answered. "A white man is regarded by the
Confederate soldiers, but all of this crew are run-away slaves. No
quarters will be shown us." Smalls tried to speed up the ship
but a rain of shells poured down. Captain Nickerson became
panic-stricken and left the pilot house. Smalls immediately took
control and steered the ship safely out of the reach of the guns.
For this act of valor he was promoted to Captain of the *Planter*.
The promotion coincided with the birth of Robert Smalls' second
daughter, Sarah Voorhees, on December 1, 1863.[14]

The courage displayed by Smalls in these various encounters
endeared him more and more to his people, and they acknowledged his worth by words and deeds. In June 1863, two hundred
and thirty black workmen fortified McGuire's Hill in Pittsburgh
and subsequently constructed a fort there. At the request of
George B. Vashon, a noted black educator in the city, the fort
was named Fort Smalls to commemorate "the heroism of Robert
Smalls" whose achievements "obtained him wide fame in the
North."[15]

Among Sea Island blacks Smalls was all but worshiped. He was
received with great ceremony by those who never wearied of
hearing him tell of his gallant services and the dangers through
which he had passed. He was their romantic hero and idol, who

[14] Rosbow, "The Abduction of the Planter," 107; also Smalls to QM
General, December 26, 1882 Records of Smalls and the *Planter*.

[15] George T. Fleming in the Pittsburgh *Gazette*, July 1, 1923; also Dennis S.
Nelson, *The Integration of the Negro in the U.S. Navy* (New York, 1951), 6.

had helped them to freedom. A widely told story described a conversation between two of Smalls' partisans:

"I tell you, Smalls is the greatest man in the world," said one to the other.

"Yes," said the other, "he is great, but not the greatest."

"Pshaw man," inquired the enthusiastic admirer, "who's greater than Smalls?"

"Why, Jesus Christ," the other replied.

"Oh, Smalls is young yet," was the response.[16]

Equally laudatory was a poetic tribute paid to Smalls by Catherine L. Tillman:

He dared, this son of Negro sires,
The thrilling deed was safely done,
And Captain Smalls, as pilot steered
The ship past fire of rebel gun,
And carried to the Union fleet
This trophy of a Negro skill,
This ship for slavery's cause designed
Must now fair freedom's end fulfill.

His wife, his children, all were then
Upon this country's altars laid;
He won! Ask you the reason why?
He was a man and not afraid.
Oh, much loved South, because our race
In greatest numbers cling to thee,
We join with thee in praise of him
Who dared so much for liberty.[17]

The accomplishments of Robert Smalls during the war, however, did not make him immune to racial discrimination while serving in the Union navy. The Seymour affair which took place sometime in 1863 was a dramatic illustration of this. Smalls had been ordered to see the Admiral on board the *Wabash.* When the boat carrying Smalls and General Seymour pulled alongside the *Wabash,* the latter hailed the officer of the day: "This *boy*

---

[16] See Woodson, "Robert Smalls and His Descendants," 28-29.
[17] Katherine L. Tillman in *Chicago Conservator,* n.d.

wants to see the Admiral. Will you please let him know that the *boy* is waiting?" He turned to Smalls and cried out in a loud voice: "Here *boy*, you can go aboard, and the officer will tell you when the officer is ready to see you." "Now, Smalls is not a boy," Charles Nordhoff, a New York reporter for *Harper's Monthly,* commented on Seymour's show of disrespect. "He is a man and wears a beard sufficient to show it. I blushed for General Seymour when I heard him use the old cant of the slave master. Because this gallant fellow happened to have a black skin, he speaks of him in a way that seemed to be contemptibly mean." He commented also that Smalls seemed "a very quiet man without the slightest swagger. How he looked or felt when he was called 'boy' in this way I cannot tell you—for I dared not look in the poor fellow's face."[18]

Nordhoff's article was printed in Northern papers and drew public attention for a time. The New York *Evening Post* blamed the defeat of General Seymour in a battle in Florida on his "virulent pro-slavery attitude" as shown by "his contemptuous treatment of Robert Smalls." The situation looked explosive, but Smalls generously came to the defense of Seymour and, with the help of his first mate, wrote a letter to the *Evening Post* stating that "from the first day of my arrival within the Union lines, General Seymour has always shown me the greatest regard, whenever in public or private inquiring how I was or if I was in need." The embarrassed General forwarded the letter to the newspaper along with correspondence of his own.[19]

The Seymour affair was settled amicably, but it appeared that Smalls' successes, especially at the expense of noted white officers like Captain Nickerson and General Seymour, excited the jealousy and anger of other white officers around him. The attention showered upon Smalls at a time when Negro inferiority was accepted as axiomatic created resentment and apparently caused attempts to deflate his reputation. Smalls' friends were not there-

[18] Charles Nordhoff, *The Freedmen of South Carolina,* typescript (New York, 1863).
[19] New York *Evening Post,* September-October 1862; Smalls to the editor of the *Evening Post;* General Seymour to the editor of the *Evening Post,* April 4, 1864; *Rebellion Records,* Vol. 8 (November 1863-May 1864).

fore surprised when, in 1864, he was ordered to take the *Planter* through waters he knew nothing about to Philadelphia. Miller maintained that the order, "if not thoughtless was most uncalled for, and is regarded by many as heartless, if not cruel." According to Miller, the "officers had intrigued" to get the order, and boasted afterward that "they would run him [Smalls] out of the service of the Navy, it being well known that he had never seen a written chart of the Atlantic Coast Line, knew nothing about Cape Hatteras, Hamptonroads, the Chesapeake Bay, or the Delaware Bay, which he had to enter to go to Philadelphia."[20] Officially, however, the *Planter* was sent to Philadelphia for repairs, the boiler, boiler feed for the donkey engine, and the exhaust pipe needing replacement.

Be this as it may, Smalls received the order with "buoyancy." He asked for three weeks' shore leave and sought the assistance of an ex-English sea captain, Colonel Elwell, to explain to him the intricacies of navigation in the Atlantic Coast. Thus informed, he left Hilton Head, and with the cooperation of good weather made the journey in three days. He entered the Delaware Bay after ten o'clock on the night of May 13, 1864, exactly two years after he had abducted the *Planter*. Once again, commented a later writer, "the fortress of prejudice had been successfully stormed.[21]

It was thought that repairs on the ship would take a few days, but, as work continued on the *Planter,* the days stretched into weeks and the weeks into months. It was nine months before the last coat of paint dried and the ship was ready to return to the South.

Whether or not Smalls spent much of his time in Philadelphia acquiring an education is not clear. Contemporary Thomas Miller indicated that, while in Philadelphia, Smalls became a student of two educated blacks in the city, Bassett and Catom, the first his teacher by day and the other by night. William Smalls, on the other hand, disputes this, and maintains that it was not until the war was over that his father acquired whatever knowledge of

---

[20] Miller, "Address," 5; Records of Smalls and the *Planter*.
[21] Sterling, *Captain of the Planter*, 144.

reading and writing he had. He credits much of this knowledge to his father's personal effort and the help of a Beaufort teacher, one Miss Cooley, whom Smalls met after the war. According to William, his father used to get up at five in the morning and study till seven when Miss Cooley came in and stayed till nine. He did this for nine months, and this was all the education he had, except the daily reading of the *Washington Star*.

While in Philadelphia, Smalls helped the abolitionists of the city in local fund-raising to aid in the work of rehabilitating the freedmen of the South. With letters of introduction from Charlotte Forten, he soon became a celebrity in the city's abolitionst circles. He addressed the General Conference of the African Methodist Episcopal Church, appealing for money to help his people in the New South improve their condition. In several places, he asked for books, clothing, and money for the freedmen.[22]

Also important was the highly publicized streetcar controversy. One day, Smalls and a friend were returning from a visit to the shipyard. When it started to rain they decided to take a streetcar back to their rooms. En route, the conductor ordered them to leave their seats and move to the open platform to make room for two white men who had boarded at the same time. Though the conductor explained that "men of their color" were not allowed in the streetcars, Smalls felt insulted and refused to move. When the conductor explained that that was the law, Smalls disembarked rather than ride on the platform.

The incident was promptly taken up by the press. Newspapers carried the story of the war hero who had been put off a Philadelphia streetcar. On December 30, 1864, the Philadelphia *Press* commented that, "while colored men, women and children are refused admittance to the cars, or expelled from the platform at the pleasure of the conductors, the worst classes of whites may ride." It was a common thing, the paper maintained, to see white men violate the rules which forbade smoking and the use of "indecent language in the presence of the ladies" with the full

22 "Captain Robert Smalls Addresses the General Conference of 1864," *A.M.E. Church Review*, January-March 1955.

knowledge of the conductors. But the rules "which excluded all colored persons" were "justified and thoroughly executed on the pretext that they protect the comfort of the passengers." The paper indicated the injustice of the situation by printing the story of Robert Smalls, "the war hero who had run a rebel vessel out of Charleston and given it to the Union fleet [and] was recently put out of a Thirteenth Street car." Fair-minded Philadelphians signed an appeal to the Boards of Presidents of the City Passenger Railways in protest. Quakers decided to boycott the cars until black passengers were admitted. A mass meeting was organized at Concert Hall at which important men like Jay Cooke, the financier, and Matthias Baldwin, the locomotive builder, were prominent speakers. Spurred on by the incident, the storm of protest grew and some of the railway companies were forced to give in. By 1867, the state legislature passed a law forbidding discrimination in public transportation.[23]

On December 17, the *Planter* left Philadelphia and reached Hilton Head without incident on December 24. On April 14, Smalls and his ship took part in the ceremonial raising of the Federal flag at Fort Sumter.

This was a day of jubilation for Union-minded South Carolinians in general, and the freed blacks of Charleston in particular. It was the fourth anniversary of the historic battle of Fort Sumter, and all the vessels that had participated in this theater of war took part in the ceremony. Senators, congressmen, generals, and such prominent abolitionists as William Lloyd Garrison and Henry Ward Beecher were present to watch this historic raising of the Federal flag.

Justus Clement French and Edward Gary, members of famous

---

[23] Philadelphia *Press,* December 30, 1864 and January 13, 1865; New Orleans *Tribune,* February 16, 1865. For accounts of the incident and its aftermath, see the following: W. E. B. Du Bois, *The Philadelphia Negro* (Philadelphia, 1899); James Kauffman, *Philadelphia Navy Yards* (New York, 1948); *Report of the Committee Appointed for the Purpose of Securing to the Colored People the Right to Use the Street Cars* (Philadelphia, 1867); Frederick Spiers, *Street Railroad System of Philadelphia* (Baltimore, 1898); William Still, *A Brief Narrative of the Struggle for the Rights of the Colored People of Philadelphia in the City Railway Cars* (Philadelphia, 1867).

abolitionist Reverend Henry Ward Beecher's Brooklyn Congregation, and passengers on the *Oceanus,* another noted ship, left
a dramatic description of that memorable incident.[24]

The flotilla of weather-beaten and war-torn vessels approached
Charleston in the thick of night. Before the party were crowds
of people, mainly black, who had gathered upon the wharves to
witness this "home-coming of heroes of many a well-fought battle."
The wharf was covered with a "motley gang of native negroes,
contrabands, poor whites, and rough-looking fellows," whose appearance was anything but an invitation to familiarity. The announcement that General Lee had surrendered was greeted with
"such a wild tumult of exultation as made the night vocal." The
local band struck-up "The Star-Spangled Banner," to which the
band of the *Oceanus* replied with "My Country 'Tis of Thee,"
followed by "Hail, Columbia!"

The morning lent added beauty to the scene. A slight shower
during the night had laid the dust and lent a delicious coolness
to the air. Only the sight of deserted houses, windows with broken
glasses, and dilapidated walls interfered with the picture of mag-
nificence. However, the air was "spiced with the aroma of flowers
and freighted with the melody of birds, all guiltless of secession,
and warbling their welcome."

Robert Smalls and the *Planter* occupied the central position in
the whole exhibition. Commenting on the position of once rich
but now impoverished Charleston planters, French and Gary
maintained that their misery ought not to be regretted because
they had lived on the "spoils of the bondmen," one of whom,
Robert Smalls, now with a salary of $1800 as the commander of
the *Planter,* "is able to give bread to half the bank presidents and
brokers of Broad Street."

The scene in the harbor was very gay. Lines of flags and signals
of every color were everywhere to be seen. Central in interest as
the vessels steamed into the harbor was the *Planter.* Her three
decks were crowded with "grey-haired old men whose wrinkles
were lighted with deep but quiet joy, middle aged men and

---

[24] *The trip of the Steamer Oceanus to Fort Sumter, April 14, 1865*
(Brooklyn, New York, 1865).

women of every grade of color possible to Southern civilization
. . . cadaverous and ragged beings holding about them their tat-
tered garments, boys and girls whose jubilation exhibited itself
in the most astonishing display of ivory." All had come to pay
public tribute and respect to the black hero of the *Planter*. Upon
the top of the wheelhouse of the ship, conspicuous to every person's view, stood Robert Smalls, "a prince among them, self-pos-
sessed, prompt and proud, and giving his orders to the helmsman
in ringing tones of command." When he was noticed by the
crowd, guns boomed, bells rang, bands played "the most enliven-
ing and patriotic airs," and men and women sang praises of this
"freedom-loving former slave."

Meanwhile, the flag of the *Planter,* seen above the parapet
waving toward the landing, was greeted with cheers. One black,
William Bradley, boomed out in baritone, "Victory at Last,"
and the multitude joined in singing this resounding song. As the
Union flag rose slowly to the top of the pole the whole multitude
rose to its feet, waved hats and handkerchiefs with frantic exultation, and "with one long pealing, deafening, ecxatic [sic] shout
of triumph," hailed the dear flag until it touched the peak. Tears
of gladness filled every eye and "flowed down cheeks unused to
weeping." Charleston, "that cradle of rebellion," had again come
under the jurisdiction of the "flag of the free heart's home and
hope."[25]

Renowned for his calmness, Smalls was overwhelmed by the
enthusiastic welcome and, for once, lost control of himself and
the *Planter*. He failed to give the signal for reversing in time and
thus allowed his ship to crash into the port wheelhouse of the
Oceanus, making both the splinters and the colors fly. "A little
less zeal and more discretion on the part of the colored Captain,"
a member of the crew maintained, would have prevented "this
momentary fright to our ladies." The ship, however, suffered no
serious damage and the event hardly dampened the festivities.

Before the organization of the Freedmen's Bureau, the *Planter*
was regularly used to transport food and other provisions for the
destitute refugees who had followed Sherman's army. Under the

command of Smalls, and with a crew of twenty-five, the vessal
assisted in the rehabilitation of the blacks displaced by the war.
On September 30, 1865, the ship formally entered the service of
the Freedmen's Bureau.

The war was over, and the Navy apparently had no more use
for the black Captain. On June 11, 1865, Smalls was ordered to
report to Baltimore for discharge from the service. In 1866, the
Planter was put out of commission and appraised by the Navy at
$15,000 of which Smalls was to receive $1500. Smalls considered
the navy appraisal too low and his share of the money too meager,
and later tried to have both reassessed. Actually, however, the
case did not meet all the conditions laid down in the prize laws
of March 3, 1849. Robert Smalls was a civilian at the time of the
capture of the vessel, and there was no precedent for paying prize
money to civilians. The controversy over Smalls' claims later became a subject for congressional investigation. In 1883, John F.
Dezendorf, Chairman of the House Committee on Naval Affairs,
brought the issue before the Congress. He had earlier taken evidence to show that, at the time of capture, the *Planter* was worth
about $60,000. He therefore argued that the previous appraisal
and Smalls' share of $1500 were "absurdly low," especially in view
of the "meritorious and praiseworthy action, calling for great
bravery and daring" of Smalls. The gallant services of Smalls, he
declared, had passed "unrecognized and badly rewarded," and he
called on the House to act on the issue. Dezendorf's argument
met with little response from his congressional colleagues. In a
later session, the issue came up again for discussion but failed to
pass.[26]

Smalls' dissatisfaction with the financial reward for his heroic
exploits did not blind him to the enormous transformations
events of the past four years had brought to his people and himself. The long debate over slavery had been terminated by the
war in which he had played such a prominent part. He himself,
heretofore an unknown slave boy, had become a courageous and
daring captain, a loyal American citizen, and, above all, a black

---

[26] *Congressional Record,* 47th Congress, 1st Session, 3437-40; also 49th Congress, 2nd Session, 289, 670; Charleston *News and Courier,* July 31, 1888.

if not a national hero. The battle for freedom had only begun, however, and when that battle moved into the political arena, Sea Island blacks turned to their "Captain Robert Smalls" for the leadership and service demanded by the Reconstruction Era.

III

POLITICAL APPRENTICESHIP

RECONSTRUCTION for the Sea Islanders began with the occupation of Port Royal by the Union forces under the command of General DuPont in November of 1861. As Port Royal area planters saw their defenses collapse before the advance of the Union forces, many became frightened and fled, leaving behind nearly ten thousand of their plantation slaves and a considerable store of corn and cotton, much of the latter unginned and still on the stalk. A large portion of the blacks who were either abandoned or refused to flee with their masters were aged, infirm, or children. So miserable were they apparently, that one Northern enthusiast, who wanted his friends to help, described them as "a people scarcely emerged from childhood, an unfortunate class of people in such a state of abject ignorance and mental stolidity as to preclude any possibility of self-government and self-maintenance in their present condition." Soon declared neither slaves nor free men but "contraband property, subject to seizure by the Federal authorities," they presented a big problem to both the government and private charity.[1]

[1] "The Freedmen of South Carolina," Address by J. M. McKim, July 9, 1862, *Rebellion Pamphlet*, 63, 1-5; Thomas D. Howard, "The Freedmen's Paradise," Charleston *News and Courier*, December 26, 1888. The legal implications of the term "contraband" are discussed by Edward Pierce in "The Contrabands at Fortress Monroe," *Atlantic Monthly*, VIII (November 1862), 627-630.

The fate of the freed slaves provoked a hot controversy between advocates of emancipation and their opponents. One abolitionist argument was that, if the slaves should be freed and paid a fair compensation for their labor, they would not constitute a public burden or nuisance because they would be as capable of supporting themselves as any class of people in the world. On their part, opponents of emancipation presented a contrary argument, and the situation in Port Royal offered an opportunity for proof of either case. Successful rehabilitation of the "contrabands" would strengthen the hands of the abolitionists while failure would certainly seriously weaken their case.[2]

The situation in Port Royal could gratify either side. Upon the arrival of the Union forces on the Islands, many of the abandoned black slaves on the plantations, either because they wanted to avoid the coming cotton harvest, or as an expression of an inward freedom, destroyed the cotton gins and other property in the area. On their part, many planters who had fled upon the arrival of the Union forces and were apparently least concerned with the real estate they were leaving behind—land, slaves, and cotton—came back under cover of darkness in the first weeks of Federal occupation to set fire to the cotton houses. It was also obvious, however, and one fugitive planter who wanted to burn his cotton fields admitted this, that the abandoned cotton in the fields and the slaves could become an asset to the invaders and the blacks themselves. The slaves could be put to work to harvest the crops and be paid for their labor.[3]

In Washington, the collection of abandoned property, including slaves and cotton, was the responsibility of the Treasury Department. Salmon P. Chase, Secretary of the Department, had emerged as a "mainspring of anti-slavery influences within the councils of the President." Because of his anti-slavery convictions, Chase seized the opportunity presented at Port Royal to test newly released slaves in the responsibilities of free laborers. Mean-

[2] See John S. Taylor, *American Liberties and American Slavery* (New York, 1838), 184-185.

[3] *The New York Times,* February 24, 1862; New York *Tribune,* November 20, 1861; Charleston *Daily Courier,* November 11, 1861. Willie Lee Rose describes the situation in great detail in *Rehearsal,* Chaps. 1 and 4.

while, public sentiment was rallying to support Chase and his group. One correspondent criticized the apparent cold attitude of the government toward the abandoned slaves at Port Royal. The capture of Port Royal, he maintained, was "a brilliant achievement," but would serve little purpose "unless the Government does aright with the institution of slavery in the region thereabout." Another man told Chase that the sentiments in northern Ohio were in favor of his posture. Thus encouraged, Secretary Chase sent Edward L. Pierce, a young Boston attorney, a personal friend and supporter, and a man strong in his anti-slavery convictions, to Port Royal in December 1861 to prepare the abandoned slaves "for self-support by their own industry hereafter." Pierce left for the Sea Islands immediately to begin "an experiment of a guided transition from slavery to freedom," later known as the Port Royal Experiment.[4]

In many ways the child of necessity, the Port Royal Experiment became the most complex, the most sophisticated, and the most realistic of the organized black communities. Conceived as a laboratory for testing the abolitionist theory of the worth of the black slaves, the Experiment tried to provide for blacks suddenly freed and thrown into circumstances for which they had had no basic training. Cotton agents, military authorities, and a band of anti-slavery men mainly from Boston, the Gideon Band, would soon come together in an effort to help the "contrabands" bridge the gap between slave and rewarding free labor. There was no doubt, wrote a correspondent for *The New York Times,* that the "negro question is destined immediately to assume in this quarter proportions and aspects utterly unlike any that it has presented elsewhere."[5]

By 1862, the Port Royal Experiment was well under way. The blacks were employed to cultivate cotton, corn, and other provisions which were exported to the North. The freedmen engaged in the enterprise were reported to be cheerful, contented, and

[4] For details see Rose, *Rehearsal,* Chap. 1.

[5] *The National Anti-Slavery Standard,* November 30, 1861 quoting *The Times.* For examples of other projects, see William and Jane H. Pease, *Black Utopia: Negro Communal Experiments in America* (Madison, Wis., 1963).

happy. Counseled by General O. O. Howard, later head of The Freedmen's Bureau, "to try hard," they eagerly seized the opportunities offered to improve their condition, especially through education. Men, women, and children hurried to the schools "at all hours and at most unseasonable times . . . expecting to catch a lesson." Driven by a deep determination "never to be made slaves again" and haunted by the fear of their masters' return, the freedmen labored to make permanent their freedom.[6]

Robert Smalls became prominent in the work of the Experiment. Success would require Northern support, and Smalls could be used effectively to gain it. The directors of the enterprise realized that Northern generosity would have to be stimulated by emotional appeals, and Smalls was admirably qualified to attract both attention and sympathy.

In October 1862, Smalls went to New York on behalf of the Experiment. There, he talked about the capabilities of black soldiers, and asked for books, schools, and clothing for the freedmen of the South. He was received with great enthusiasm in churches and other public places. The trip was climaxed by a public reception arranged by the Reverend Highland Garnet, a leading black minister and orator. Nearly all the prominent black people of New York and Brooklyn were present. According to the New York *Evening Post:*

> The spectacle of a great and intelligent gathering of black men and women to do special honor to a recognized hero, who had honored, not only himself, but his race, was sufficiently sublime. The entire audience, as he was recognized, rose and received him with demonstrations of extreme delight. The period of the reception and its object, with the new light the congregation felt was dawning on their race, combined to intensify the welcome and to impart to the enthusiastic outbursts of feelings which were manifested an electrifying effect that can scarcely be conceived.

Smalls was given a medal showing the *Planter* leaving Charleston harbor. On the reverse side of the medal was inscribed: PRESENTED

[6] Elizabeth Bothume, *First Days Among the Contrabands* (Boston, 1893), 22, 35, 68.

TO ROBERT SMALLS BY THE COLORED CITIZENS OF NEW YORK, OCTOBER
2, 1862, AS A TOKEN OF THEIR REGARD FOR HIS HEROISM, HIS LOVE OF
LIBERTY, AND HIS PATRIOTISM.[7]

Back in Beaufort, the love of freedom exhibited by Smalls in
abducting the *Planter* was held up as an example to the Sea
Islanders, and this helped in local fund-raising. The Reverend
Mansfield French, well-known minister and teacher of the Sea
Island blacks, would not end a Sunday sermon without reminding his congregation of the enormous responsibilities they faced
as free men and of the dangers Smalls had gone through to get
his own freedom. On certain Sundays, he would introduce Smalls,
who would then proceed to give a full account of his escape with
the *Planter*. Such occasions always ended with an appeal for
funds to help in the education and employment of the freedmen.[8]

Robert Smalls himself very early manifested an interest in the
education of the Sea Islanders, and this was to remain one of his
major preoccupations. In 1867, at a government tax sale, Smalls
purchased a two-story building containing eight large rooms and
a chapel, and deeded it "to the colored children of the town
[Beaufort] to be held in trust for them." The property was subsequently converted into a school for black children, and Smalls
was elected president of the board of trustees. In this capacity he
undertook many speaking tours to the North to appeal for funds,
books, and equipment for the school. Mrs. Hannah Smalls, treasurer of the Ladies Fair of Beaufort, a voluntary association formed to advance the social life of the area, joined in several appeals
to Northerners for funds. It is not surprising, therefore, that
Smalls' contemporaries credited much of the educational advance-
ment of the area to his efforts. Irving Washington, a black educator, attributed to Smalls the attraction to the area of such
prominent teachers as Jennie W. Lynch and Charlotte Forten.
"He saw the necessity of educating his people, though not himself educated," Washington wrote. "His efforts were successful

---

[7] New York *Evening Post,* October 12, 1862; the medal is in the possession
of Mrs. Elizabeth Hall of Washington, D.C.
[8] *The National Anti-Slavery Standard,* September 20, 1862.

and resulted . . . in the betterment of the conditions, mentally, morally and religiously, of the people."[9]

In addition, Smalls displayed a financial skill which made him an example to many a property-conscious Sea Islander. At a government auction sale in 1864, he bought the Prince Street house of Henry McKee where he had spent the earliest years of his life. In the spring of 1866, he joined a cooperative venture, the Star and Spangled Association, which, under the leadership of Tom Long, a black veteran of the First South Carolina Volunteers, raised $20,000 by $15 to $100 subscriptions and acquired a steamer to operate along the coast under the command of Robert Smalls. Between 1866 and 1868, Smalls made extensive purchases of land and buildings in Beaufort and around the islands. In 1871, he bought the Beaufort County poor farm, a town house in Port Royal, and some town lots, several of them at auction sales resulting from court suits he instigated against some of his political rivals. He added "acre to acre and house to house," a hostile newspaper later complained, "kept race horses for his pleasure and drove about in his elegant barouche."[10] Many political rivals later complained about Smalls' ostentatiousness, but to many blacks in the area his property holdings established Smalls as a member of the small but important middle class into which most of them aspired to enter. Moreover, by sponsoring educational projects from which the people profited, Smalls identified his economic successes with the needs of his poor constituents. The Beaufort black community continued to recognize his leadership in various ways, including a song, "The Negro Boatman," which was very popular with the children of the district.

Meanwhile, however, some national developments also affected the Port Royalists. The Sea Islanders received the Emancipation Proclamation with great jubilation. Like the blacks of Boston described by Frederick Douglass, they sang the anthem, "Sound the loud timbrel o'er Egypt's dark sea, Jehovah hath triumphed, his

---

[9] *The Liberator,* September 12, 1862; *Palmetto Post,* October 23, 1884; *Weekly Anglo-American,* August, 1865; Washington, "General Robert Smalls," 8.
[10] Beaufort *Free South,* January 23, 1864; *The New York Times,* April 2, and June 11, 1866; Beaufort *Republican,* November 3, 1872.

people are free." Rufus Saxton, regarded by the Sea Islanders as one of the three greatest men in the world (the others were President Lincoln and Robert Smalls), later recalled the emotions of the blacks of the Sea Islands in this "their year of jubilee." Never in all his rounds did "the glad sun shine upon a scene of more dramatic power and beauty. . . . What a day of promise that was!" However dimly they understood the proclamation, some far-sighted Sea Islanders realized that political action would be necessary to consolidate their freedom.[11]

By the spring of 1864, therefore, the Sea Islanders made their debut in national politics. They conceived the idea of sending a full contingent of delegates to the Republican National Convention at Baltimore in June. On May 18, they held a rally at Beaufort. There was some tension at this meeting, which was attended equally by blacks and whites, and for a time "white paired off against black." A timely speech by Reuben Tomlinson, a former Philadelphia bank clerk, a young man of "good anti-slavery principles" who had come out to Port Royal as a superintendent and would later play an important role in Republican politics in the area, restored order. Sixteen delegates, including Robert Smalls, and three other blacks were chosen.[12]

At the convention the members received seats on the floor, but were denied official representation and were not acknowledged by the chairman. Efforts to bring the question of black suffrage before the convention were adroitly circumvented. Editor Thompson of the Beaufort *Free South,* later to become disenchanted by the freedmen, commented that "all were ready to have the negro fight for the Union, die for it, but were hardly ready to have him vote for it."[13]

Some observers laughed at the presumption of the Port Royal citizens who yearned for political recognition. The delegation was satirically referred to as "three or four army sutlers sand-

[11] *Life and Times of Frederick Douglass Written by Himself* (New York, 1941), 387-389; Saxton to Smalls, December 25, 1871, cited in Beaufort *Republican,* January 4, 1872.

[12] Pearson, *Letters from Port Royal,* 262-268.

[13] Beaufort *Free South,* July 2, 1864; also W. E. B. Du Bois, *Black Reconstruction in America* (New York, 1935), 230; *Letters from Port Royal,* 262-268.

wiched among contrabands." William C. Gannet, a young teacher from Boston, in his diary, May 19, 1864, complained that the whole affair was premature and foolish. It would appear, however, that the affair was not without significance. The South Carolina flag created a sensation at Baltimore, and many distinguished citizens from all sections of the Union were attracted by the delegation. Great interest was manifested in the work of reorganization in progress in the Sea Islands. Moreover, the delegates took advantage of their proximity to Washington to bring to the attention of appropriate officials there the need for civil courts in Beaufort. They also asked for the trade restrictions still in effect to be lifted.[14]

For Smalls and his black colleagues, the episode must have been significant in other ways. The denial of official recognition indicated clearly that emancipation had not brought the much desired equality with the whites. Obviously, the fight for freedom was far from over, and the former slaves would have to seek political influence. Long before the Union League, the Freedmen's Bureau, and the more radical programs of 1866-67, the Negroes had recognized the Republican Party, the "party of Lincoln," as the party that gave them freedom. Also, the choice of Smalls as a delegate showed that the community had designated him as a political leader for the difficult years ahead.[15]

Meanwhile, in the Sea Islands events were taking a dramatic turn. As Sherman's army advanced into Georgia, more and more "contrabands" poured into the islands, and even before any of these arrived, the black population of the area had swollen to well over 15,000 by 1864. The *National Freedmen* reported that Sherman's refugees kept arriving at the rate of nearly a hundred each day. These were added burden to the lean stores of the Department, which, however, continued to provide employment, food, clothes, and medicine. On January 16, 1865, Sherman, with the full concurrence of the Secretary of War, issued his Special Field Order Number 15. The whole of the Sea Island region from Charleston southward to the St. Johns River, and the coastal

14 Beaufort *Free South,* July 2, 1864, referring to statements of others about the delegation; Pearson, *Letters from Port Royal,* 268; Rose, *Rehearsal,* 317.
15 See Rose, *Rehearsal,* 317-318.

lands thirty miles to the interior, were designated for exclusive black settlement. All "abandoned property" could be taken up by the refugees from the interior in tracts not exceeding forty acres. They were to be protected in their occupation of these lands and receive "possessory" titles until such a time as they could protect themselves, or until Congress should regulate their titles. General Saxton was appointed Inspector of Settlements and Plantations and was charged with the responsibility of colonizing Sherman's refugees. Also, the presence of the soldiers afforded a ready market for the products of the islanders, and the camps provided work at high wages for some.[16]

But even in the midst of these encouraging conditions, the Sea Islanders had reasons to be dissatisfied. The prosperity in which they found themselves was largely delusive, for it was the prosperity of war times. After the war, Sea Island cotton planters faced a series of crop failures because of "want of manure, careless working" and great damage done by the boll weevil. The health of the blacks was also far from satisfactory. "The poor Negroes die as fast as ever," teacher Laura Towne commented. "The children are all emaciated to the last degree. . . . It is frightful to see such suffering among children." Also, even though the army of liberation provided a market for their products, the blacks were often cheated and abused by the soldiers. For a time General Saxton was forced to place Beaufort out of bounds for the freedmen for their own protection. After the war, the freedmen faced the possibility of being evicted from the lands given them by Sherman's order and this caused great consternation among them. General Howard described the reaction of the freedmen at a meeting in a large Episcopal Church on Edisto Island, held in late October 1865, to discuss the issue. When the order returning most of the land to the former owners was presented to them, the announcement was greeted with "no apparent favor." Asked to sing while their representatives and the officers negotiated on the proposals, one black asked "How can we sing the Lord's song in a strange land?" When eventually they were pre-

16 *Official Records*, 1, XLVII, Part II, 60-62; also the *National Freedmen* (April 1865), 1.

vailed upon to sing, a "sweet-voiced" black woman began the hymn: "Nobody knows the trouble I feel—nobody but Jesus." When the terms were announced, the people cried their disapproval and their "eyes flashed unpleasantly." A strong man called out from the gallery, "Why, General Howard, why do you take away our lands? You take them from us who have always been true, always true to the government! You give them to our all-time enemies. That is not right!"[17]

Even some of the Northern "philanthropists" did not fail to exploit the blacks when it suited their interest. "You can not know how amusing it is to see in our letters of this time any words about 'philanthropy,' 'noble mission,' 'glorious work,' " wrote one of them in 1864. "We are speculators now, we are making money out of the negroes' ill paid labor. We have little reputation except for prosperous selfishness."[18]

The initial events in the state and the country seemed promising. Before the Amnesty Proclamation of May 29, 1865, the government of the United States acting through its military officers exercised full control over South Carolina, and this gave the blacks much reason for optimism. By an order dated May 15, 1865, it was emphasized that the "people of the black race are free citizens of the United States" whose rights were to be respected accordingly. The Freedmen's Bureau promoted, formulated, and supervised contracts between landlords and their former slaves. Blacks could also look forward to the troops in the garrison for protection as more and more of their own people were showing up in uniforms.

By September 1865, however, things were different. Following the May Amnesty, Benjamin Perry was selected provisional governor for South Carolina with authority to prescribe as soon as

---

[17] Guion Griffis Johnson, *A Social History of the Sea Islands* (Durham, N.C., 1930), 195; Pearson, *Letters from Port Royal*, 197-198; Rupert S. Holland, ed., *Letters and Diary of Laura M. Towne* (Cambridge, 1912), 153-154; Oliver Otis Howard, *Autobiography* (2 vols., New York, 1908), I, 238-239; also Records of the Direct Tax Commission for the District of South Carolina, Bureau of Internal Revenue, Group 58, United States Treasury Department, National Archives, Washington, D.C.

[18] William Gannet to Catherine Tilden, March 9, 1864; William Channing Gannet Papers, University of Rochester.

possible the proper rules and regulations necessary for convening a convention composed of the "loyal portion" of the state for drawing up a constitution to restore the state to its rightful place in the Union. The all-white convention met on September 13, and drew up a constitution which, among other things, prohibited slavery and involuntary servitude "except as punishment for a crime whereof the party shall have been duly convicted." More ominous, however, the convention appointed a commission to prepare and report to the legislature at its first session "what laws would be necessary and proper in consequence of the alterations made in the fundamental law, and especially to prepare and submit a code for the regulation of labor and protection and government" of the black population of the state.[19]

This report was submitted to the General Assembly, which established laws to regulate the relations of "persons of color" to the state government and to the white race. The laws conferred on "persons of color" the right to acquire, own, and dispose of property and to make contracts and enjoy the fruits of their labors. They could sue and be sued and could receive protection under the law in their persons and property. However, it was noted that "persons of color" were not entitled to social and political equality with white persons. Willful homicide, assault upon a white woman with manifest intent to ravish her, and sexual intercourse with any white woman were punishable with death. A black could be whipped or imprisoned for assaulting a white employer or any member of his family. They were to constitute no part of the state militia, and could not own or keep firearms, a sword, or any military weapon without permission. The district court was clothed with exclusive jurisdiction, subject to appeal, of all cases involving blacks. Finally, the code forbade blacks to engage in any trade or business other than husbandry and farming or domestic service, except under a license requiring a substantial annual fee.[20]

The merits and demerits of these "Black Codes," as they soon

[19] J. S. Reynolds, *Reconstruction in South Carolina, 1865-1877* (Columbia, S.C., 1905), 17-27.
[20] W. L. Fleming, *Documentary History of Reconstruction* (2 vols., Cleveland, Ohio, 1906-7), I, 298 for text.

came to be called, have been the subject of much historical controversy.[21] For the black leaders, however, it was clear from the codes that economic and political power in the state still remained in the hands of the shaken but far-from-crushed former slave-holding class. Worse still, the Johnson Administration in Washington had apparently accepted this subtle attempt to reestablish white control, and to have abandoned the freedmen. The New York *Journal of Commerce* expressed an apparently widely held sentiment in the nation. "The future depends now on the free will of the negro and not on orders or laws," the paper wrote on May 24, 1865. "No military power can save them." The evolving labor system was also cause for alarm. Army officer Leonard B. Perry complained about the insertion, in some of the contracts signed between freedmen and planters, of a clause establishing a system of peonage by which the freedmen were forced to bind themselves to work out any debt they might incur to their employers. (A black writer, Lafayette Hershaw, has explained that the real foundation of peonage, as it relates to the black man, "is the refusal to regard him as a man having rights as others have them.") In an editorial on June 29, 1865, even the generally unsympathetic Charleston *Daily Courier* cried out against the neglect of the poor freedmen. "We who live in a Christian country," the paper maintained, "must do as Christians did."[22]

Deserted by the Johnson government, and oppressed by the whites of South Carolina, many of the blacks resigned themselves to the situation. Some signed labor contracts if only to keep themselves from starving while others migrated from the state. This

[21] Generally, pro-Southern historians maintain that the "Black Codes" represented an attempt to curb the excesses and lawlessness of blacks. Another school, however, sees in the laws an attempt by the South either to re-enslave the freedmen or put them in a position very near to slavery. For the first view, see the following: William Dunning, *Reconstruction: Political and Economic, 1865-1877* (New York, 1962), 54-59; James Ford Rhodes, *History of the United States* (8 vols., London, New York, 1900-1909), V, 556; Reynolds, *Reconstruction in South Carolina*, 17-25. For the other view see Altheus Taylor, *The Negro in South Carolina During Reconstruction, 1865-1877* (New York, 1966), 80.

[22] Charleston *Daily Courier*, June 28 and 29, 1865; L. M. Hershaw, *Peonage* (Washington, D.C., 1915), 11.

state of affairs, however, was not acceptable to the black leaders. They gathered in a convention in Charleston on November 20, 1865, to make their feelings known.

The convention, presided over by Thomas M. Holmes of Charleston, rejected the proposals of colonization or flight, welcomed the support of white allies, and protested vehemently against unfair labor practices, violence, peonage, and restrictions upon land ownership. In an Address of the State Convention to the White Citizens of South Carolina written by R. H. Cain, a black Charleston minister and newspaper publisher, they declared:

> We simply ask that we shall be recognized as men; that there shall be no obstructions placed in our way; that the same laws which govern white men shall govern black men; that schools be established for the education of colored children as well as white, and that the advantages of both colors shall, in this respect, be equal; that no impediments be put in our way of acquiring homesteads for ourselves and our people; that, in short, we be dealt with as others are—in equity and justice.[23]

Obviously, these demands were entirely consistent with the most basic American conceptions. The freedmen were merely asking for things which were essential for their transformation from slavery to freedom. Land, education, a secure economic situation, and the right to vote, which was not only the mark of a free man but also a necessary instrument for the attainment of economic opportunity and legal justice, were all they asked for. As Charles Crowe has observed, "while grievances against former masters may have lingered, they were more than balanced by the common desire for a free and peaceful life on terms of mutual goodwill with the white people."[24]

[23] Cited in Herbert Aptheker, *A Documentary History of the Negro People in the United States* (2 vols., New York, 1967), II, 546.

[24] For a discussion of the priorities in black demands, see Elsie Lewis, "The Political Mind of the Negro," *Journal of Southern History*, XXI (1955), 189-202; August Meier, "Negroes in the First and Second Reconstruction," *Civil War History* (August 1967), 114-130. Charles Crowe, ed., *The Age of Civil War and Reconstruction* (Illinois, 1966), 316.

These demands went unheeded by both state and Johnson administrations. In Washington, the Freedmen's Bureau Bill and the Civil Rights Bill were vetoed and even the Fourteenth Amendment was opposed by the President. Though these were passed over his vetoes, the President's opposition encouraged the South to violate them. The blacks were lucky that in his stubbornness and inability to placate Congress and Northern public opinion, Johnson "fumbled away power."[25]

The triumph of the Radicals over President Johnson in Washington was essentially a triumph for the blacks and their sympathizers. The Reconstruction Acts passed between 1866 and 1868 inaugurated a period of black political power which lasted till 1876 in South Carolina. The first indication of the new situation was seen in the formation of the constitutional convention of the state which began meeting in Columbia on June 14, 1868.[26]

Given the opportunity, the blacks acted quickly. In large numbers they enrolled in the Union League, which, founded in Philadelphia in 1862 to stimulate and promote support for the Union cause in the Civil War, was becoming an important instrument for educating blacks in their political rights and recruiting them for the Republican party. In a Republican convention held in Columbia on July 24, 1867, no less than sixty-four of the eighty delegates were blacks. They declared for universal suffrage, reorganization of the courts, the division and sale of unoccupied land among the poorer classes, and the cautious restorations of the rights of those lately guilty of treason. They called for uniform free compulsory education and a vast internal improvements program, and pledged their steadfast loyalty to the Union Republican party.[27]

On October 17, 1867, the Headquarters of the Second Military

[25] For this view of the conflict between Andrew Johnson and the Radicals, see Eric McKitrick, *Andrew Johnson and Reconstruction* (Chicago, 1960).

[26] For text see Statutes at Large, XIV, 428. For a critical evaluation of the many and varied viewpoints on Radical motivation in supporting black franchise, see LaWanda and John Cox, "Negro Suffrage and Republican Politics," *Journal of Southern History*, XXXIII (1967).

[27] *The New York Times*, July 31, 1867; Aptheker, *Documentary History*, II, 559.

District in Charleston ordered that an election be held in the state between 19 and 20 November. All the registered voters of the state would vote for or against a convention, and also for delegates to constitute such a convention, should a majority vote for the convention. The registration list was to be revised in accordance with the provisions of the Acts of Congress, and all necessary steps taken to ensure the fairness of the election. When completed, the registration list showed 47,171 whites and 80,379 blacks. On election day it was observed that blacks thronged to the polls while many whites considered it prudent to stay away. Reports reaching Charleston indicated that the elections were peaceful and quiet. In Columbia, "utmost quiet and order prevailed at the polls. The voting was confined mainly to the colored population, whose general conduct on the occasion is deserving of special praise." In all, 71,046 turned out to vote, with 68,768 voting for and 2278 against holding the convention. In Beaufort, Robert Smalls' district, of the 7824 registered voters, 4200 turned out to vote. The division was 4118 for and only two against holding the convention.[28]

Robert Smalls was one of the delegates elected from Beaufort. On March 26, 1867, he joined thirty-seven other blacks and three whites to organize a Beaufort Republican Club, the first in South Carolina. The club itself had called for a Republican state convention to meet in May to officially launch the party in the state and to select a complete slate of candidates for a constitutional convention. Smalls had served as a registrar for Beaufort County, and Sea Island blacks considered him the smartest black man in the state.[29]

On November 25, 1867, the *Daily Courier*, echoing the sentiments of many white South Carolinians, described the convention about to assemble as "representative purely of the black race, misguided as to their true welfare, and about two hundred of the white race, few of whom owe any allegiance to our soil and people." The paper declared that to call this a convention of the

[28] Charleston *Daily Courier*, October 18, 30, and November 21, 1867; also April 9, 1868.

[29] Beaufort *Tribune*, March 27, 1867; Beaufort *Republican*, October 24, 1872.

people of South Carolina was "a farce that deceives no one."[30] Actually, however, an analysis of the convention delegates on the basis of previous residence does not bear out the *Courier's* claim. Of the one hundred and twenty-four delegates, forty-eight whites and seventy-six blacks, twenty-three whites and forty-nine blacks were permanent residents of South Carolina. The *Courier* may not yet have been ready to recognize "the black race" as citizens of the state.

Despite serious opposition vocally expressed by the *Courier* and other white papers in the state, the delegates gathered in the Clubhouse on King Street in Charleston, January 14, 1868, at a convention to restore "our state to her proper relations with the Federal Union." Welcoming the delegates, Thomas J. Robertson, who took the chair on the first day, appealed to them "to frame a just and liberal constitution that will guarantee equal rights to all, regardless of race, color or previous condition."[31] A revolution was certainly in the making for South Carolina where the concept of racial equality of white and blacks was heretofore anathema.

The role of Smalls in the convention is difficult to assess since most of the discussions and negotiations outside the meeting room were not recorded, and in the convention itself Smalls apparently did not speak often. From the way he voted, the few debates he participated in, and the one important resolution he introduced, it is clear that he was concerned equally with the social, economic, and political rights of black people in South Carolina.

He was vitally concerned with a proposed homestead law which sought to exempt from any court action for debt homesteads in the country, "consisting of one hundred acres, and dwellings and appurtenances thereon to be selected by the owner thereof." Black delegates supported the resolution on the grounds that it would afford protection to the "unfortunate debtor." Other delegates, particularly the white creditors, opposed the proposal,

30 Charleston *Daily Courier,* November 25, 1867; documents in *Journal of Negro History* (1920), 63-125.
31 *Proceedings of the Constitutional Convention of the State of South Carolina, 1868* (Charleston, 1868) , 6.

however, with charges that it was retroactive and impaired the obligation of the right of contract. A heated discussion ensued and it looked like the convention would break up on this issue. Smalls, however, would not give in, and when the convention reconvened on the following day he reintroduced the proposal and asked for speedy action. The debates were resumed, and the proposal was finally passed with Smalls' support.[32]

Predictably, Smalls voted for an ordinance nullifying all contracts involving slavery. The judiciary committee had reported on an ordinance to annul the slave contracts and other liabilities where the money had not been paid. As one would expect, the recently freed slaves in the convention spoke bitterly against the recognition of any "Negro bonds." "The institution of American slavery," they argued, "never was a legal institution" and "persons held as slaves were men in every sense of the definition of man." The white delegates, especially L. S. Langley and C. C. Bowen, argued against the passage of such an ordinance and pleaded that "the only question is the condition of a mortgage at common law . . . and a conditional sale of property." Passions should not be put aside, they argued, and the matter should be looked upon as "purely a question of law." People like Robert Smalls, however, could not be expected to put aside passions in an issue that touched the very fact of their being. They argued that a formal repudiation was absolutely necessary because the bonds violated the fundamental principle of moral law expressed in the Declaration of Independence. Smalls joined his black colleagues in nullifying the "Negro bonds."[33]

Smalls also voted for relief in different forms to the people of the state. He supported a resolution requesting exemption from levy or sale "for a period of four months, one hundred acres of land, which now, or which may, prior to the expiration of the four months be under execution." He voted for a petition to the Federal administration to help South Carolina alleviate "the people's homeless and landless condition" by providing a loan from the national Treasury to enable them to buy farms at

---

32 *Proceedings,* 452, 466, 481.
33 *Ibid.,* 239-248.

reasonable credit. He also supported a petition to Congress to make an appropriation of one million dollars from the Freedmen's Bureau fund as a direct subsidy to the people to purchase land.[34]

The subject of the political disability of those "lately in rebellion" brought much controversy in the convention, and Smalls' stand on this issue should be noted. Contrary to expectation, and perhaps indicating their largesse of spirit, blacks in the state generally wished to see the political disability of the people of the state removed because this would make for "the growth and prosperity of this state, and the well-being of all men." In the convention, black delegate R. C. De Large offered a resolution to petition Congress to remove all political disabilities from citizens of the state. Black delegate Francis Cardozo, the principal of the Avery Institute in Charleston, an expert accountant and a brilliant administrator who would successively serve the state as secretary of state (1868-1872) and treasurer (1872-1877), considered it a matter of expediency as well as policy to act with generosity on this issue, arguing that his party should "exercise a generosity and magnanimity unparalled in the history of the world." As for the black delegates, this was an opportunity for them to show that, "although our people have been oppressed and have every inducement to seek revenge, although deprived of education and learning," they could rise above "all selfishness and exhibit a christian universality of spirit." A few dissenting black voices, however, argued that giving an enemy such a substantial weapon would be unsound policy.[35]

Robert Smalls was a moderate on the issue, first voting against the main resolution requiring indiscriminate removal of disabilities from all citizens of the state. He afterward supported a substitute resolution to request the Congress to remove disabilities from such citizens "as may petition for same after the adoption of the constitution," provided such citizens swore to support both the state and the United States constitutions.

Significantly, too, Smalls refused to vote on the question of

---

[34] *Ibid.*, 148, 438-439; 196-197.
[35] *Ibid.*, 877-878; Aptheker, *Documentary History*, II, 546.

striking out a provision in the Bill of Rights which defined treason as any action which negated the state constitution or helped
enemies of the same. One white delegate pleaded that, if passed,
the clause would make every prominent white man in South
Carolina a traitor, and the convention voted overwhelmingly to
strike out the clause.

Smalls' stand on these issues which vitally affected the interest
of South Carolina whites can hardly be interpreted as hatred of
the former ruling class. Political ambition, personal pique against
the traditional ruling elite, and a justifiable apprehension of
what the return to politics of this group might bring, are better
explanations for Smalls' actions. In the convention, he cheered
a fellow freedman who said: "We must unite with our white
fellow citizens. Can we afford to lose from the councils of state
our first men? No, fellow citizens, no! We want only the best and
the ablest men. And then with a strong pull, and a long pull,
and a pull together, up goes South Carolina." In fact, Smalls
became the least objectionable to the whites of the freedmen
political leaders.[36]

Smalls also disagreed with his fellow blacks on other issues,
most importantly on a debate over a one-dollar poll tax to support education which touched on suffrage. A report submitted
by the committee on education stated that "no person shall be
deprived of the right of suffrage for non-payment of the poll
tax." The provision was to ensure that black people, who were
generally the poorest in the state, would not be deprived of the
franchise for inability to pay the one-dollar-a-year poll tax.
Cardozo summed up the motivating force behind the provision
when he argued that "just as certain as you strike out that proviso, you strike at the freedmen of South Carolina. . . . There will
scarcely be a white man in the state but will be able to raise a
dollar from our enemies." The proviso was also connected with
the success of the Republican party in the state. By striking out
the provision, F. J. Moses, a white delegate and later to become
governor of the state, argued, power would again go into the

36 *Ibid.*, 338; Holland, *Towne Letters and Diary*, 240-242.

hands of the "aristocratic elements." He reminded wavering Republicans of what would happen to the party should the provision fail to pass. "If you are willing to sell out the Republican party, do it now; do not wait to go through the coming campaign. On the success of the Republican party depends your political and civil salvation for years to come." He believed the "freedmen would rather die first than yield up their votes to the Democratic party.[37]

Neither the weight of this argument nor the provision's overwhelming support persuaded Smalls to vote. It is not clear why he acted in this way. The provision was certainly to the advantage of his people and party, and his continued presence in the political arena of the state depended on the success of these groups. Though Smalls was not in favor of disfranchising any citizen of the state, he may have felt that adequate funds for the educational purposes of the state required this incentive for everyone to contribute a dollar. Education was very dear to Smalls.

Smalls also exhibited his independence in the hot debate over the tenure of office bill. This bill would provide a four-year term for the governor and the secretary of state of South Carolina. Advocates argued that such a long tenure was essential for laying the foundations of a stable government in such troubled times. Republicans generally also saw a four-year term as important for establishing their party on a firm basis. Once this was done, they maintained, "there was no power under heaven that could stop them from advancing thereafter." Some black Republicans, however, objected to the proposal, and argued that, "if we get bad men in office, we will be sure to rob the people of their rights" since impeachment was a difficult thing. In his characteristic witty manner, Smalls wondered whether those who were advocating a long tenure of office were not themselves candidates for the offices. The house rocked with laughter when Smalls indicated that the principal advocate of the proposal had in fact already announced his candidacy for office. He joined the majority

[37] *Ibid.*, 733-735.

in voting for a two-year term with the understanding that a competent officer could be honored with re-election.[38]

Small's most significant contribution to the new constitution was his resolution on education. Though the subject of a common school system to be funded by the Freedmen's Bureau had been introduced by another delegate, it remained for Smalls to call for a system of state-supported free compulsory education. The maintenance of an intelligent government, "faithful to the interests and liberties of the people," Smalls declared in the preamble to his resolution, depended "in great measure on the intelligence of the people themselves." Besides, the experience of those states which had "opened to the poor and the rich alike the opportunities of instruction" had demonstrated the utility of common schools in "elevating the intellectual character of their population." Smalls, therefore, called for an article from the educational committee providing for a system of common schools "of different grades, to be opened without charge to all classes of the people." To make this system effective, he suggested compulsory attendance for at least six months of each year for all children between the ages of seven and fourteen. Parents who failed to send their children to school should be punished, and permission for any absence was to be given by "some legal authority, appointed to direct and superintend the public schools."[39]

The "compulsory clause" in Smalls' resolution evoked heated debate from the delegates. Some white delegates criticized it as being "unrepublican and impractical." One opposed it because it negated the fact that man was "a free agent who should be so treated and regarded." Black delegates, on the other hand, were understandably very enthusiastic about the resolution. One argued that "in proportion to the education of the people so is their progress in civilization." In the end, Smalls' resolution in a slightly modified form was incorporated into the new constitution. Where Smalls had called for six months of compulsory attendance yearly, the constitution provided for "compulsory attendance at either public or private schools of all children be-

38 *Ibid.*, 765-767.
39 *Ibid.*, 100.

tween the ages of six and sixteen, not physically or mentally disabled, for a term equivalent to twenty-four months."[40]

Despite its obvious value, the educational provision of the new constitution, largely Smalls' creation, drew much opposition from contemporaries, and later became a subject for disagreement among South Carolina historians. The *Daily Courier* objected to the new constitution, among other things because of the "stupendous school arrangement requiring an enormous taxation to be borne mainly by one class for the benefit of the other." South Carolina's official Reconstruction historian, John Reynolds, denounced the educational provision as being contrary to the genius and spirit of republican institutions. A later historian, on the other hand, David Duncan Wallace, doubtless influenced by the popular acceptance of common schools in his times, hailed the educational provision as the most admirable in the constitution.[41]

As Robert Smalls himself said, the formation and running of an intelligent government requires educated children. Yet the educational level of South Carolina blacks who found themselves now saddled with the responsibility of running the state government was pitifully low. Slavery and education were clearly incompatible, and at the time of their emancipation only 5 per cent of the black population had acquired some knowledge of reading and writing. Toward the end of the war, the Freedmen's Bureau had also come to help in the educational endeavors, heretofore carried out by voluntary agencies from the North, by opening day, night, Sunday, and industrial schools. By mid-October, there were about 20,000 pupils enrolled in Bureau and other voluntary schools in the state.

From the beginning, however, many South Carolina whites had been bitterly opposed to the education of blacks, and when the Northern agents tried to teach, opposition sometimes took a violent form. In 1866, a group of white men in Lexington inter-

[40] *Ibid.*, 68, 685, 689.
[41] Charleston *Daily Courier*, April 9, 1868; Reynolds, *Reconstruction in South Carolina*, 92; David D. Wallace, *The South Carolina Constitutional Convention of 1895* Bulletin of the University of South Carolina, No. 197 (February 15, 1929), 25.

rupted a night school for blacks and threatened violence upon the son of the teacher. Despite the opposition, the eagerness of blacks to secure an education mounted. "It was a whole race trying to go to school," one black educator commented, "few were too young, and none too old, to make the attempt to learn." Smalls' resolution was an attempt to provide for anyone willing to learn.[42]

In practice, Smalls' educational provision was disappointing because the "compulsory clause" was not put into effect until the constitution was overturned in 1895. Nevertheless, the legislation was admirable. "Good citizenship," Frederick Jackson Turner once wrote, "is the end for which public schools exist." Even Wade Hampton, the redeemer governor who set out to purge the South Carolina government of all taints of Republicanism after the overthrow of the Reconstruction government, subscribed to the importance of continuing the educational policies of the radicals. In an address at the Winnebago Fair in September 1877, Hampton admitted that "we cannot afford to yield up our educational institutions for upon them devolves the duty of moulding the minds of the Southern youth." Tragically, however, South Carolina neglected its great opportunity and thus left unsolved one of its teething problems. The language of the preamble to Smalls' resolution speaks volumes for his idea of the ingredients of a good government.[43]

On March 14, 1868, the convention adjourned. Its constitution was submitted to the people and overwhelmingly endorsed despite a vituperative campaign by the *News and Courier* and other conservative white papers. The new constitution placed no racial restrictions upon suffrage, provided for the popular election of important state officers, and called for the establishment of a system of free public schools. "Despite its unsavory origin," one historian argued, "the fact that the constitution of 1868 lasted twenty-seven years, and was amended only twelve times, and seldom in matters of great importance, shows that it was suited

42 *The Nation*, I (December 1865), 779; *The New York Times*, May 25, 1866; Williamson, *After Slavery*, 208-210.

43 Frederick J. Turner, *Selected Essays: Frontier and Section* (New York, 1965), 21; Charleston *News and Courier*, September 18, 1877.

to those who lived under it, both in the wisdom of its general provisions . . . and in the freedom that it allowed the legislature to meet its problems."[44]

The convention reaffirmed that Smalls was well qualified to serve his people. Though one does not see here the oratory and eloquence associated with him in later years, it was obvious that he was an intelligent listener and could speak convincingly when necessary. His resolution on education was a landmark in the history of South Carolina. On this formal occasion to serve his people politically, Smalls completely justified their confidence. He had also shown himself to be a man of flexibility and discretion as well as conviction. Members of the convention recognized his worth by appointing him a member of the nine-man committee on finance. His people would turn to him to represent them in the first legislature under the new constitution.

[44] Wallace, *Constitutional Convention,* 26.

IV

A RADICAL BLACK REPUBLICAN

THE FIERCE CAMPAIGN carried out by the Charleston *Daily Courier* and other conservative papers against "the black and tan convention" and the generally hostile reception given to the constitution framed by that body convinced the black leaders that all was not well. The machinery which produced the new constitution, the *Daily Courier* declared, was "illegal and Revolutionary." Besides, continued the paper, the constitution was "based on the falsehood that white and blacks are the same," and it destroyed "our admirable judiciary" and "disfranchised our best citizens." The paper reminded South Carolina whites that "worse than all these we are menaced with negro rule and supremacy at the point of the sword and bayonet." "You have been suddenly put in position to exercise certain powers," a state Democratic convention warned the blacks, "the abuse of which may result disastrously to you and us. It is impossible that your present power can endure whether you use it for good or evil."[1] Such utterances left the black leaders in no doubt that the new situation was entirely unacceptable to the whites and would be reversed if not jealously guarded. Moreover, viewing the promises of tomorrow through the performances of yesterday, the black leaders could

1 Charleston *Daily Courier,* April 6 and 9, 1868.

only remember an immediate past marked by aroused expecta-
tions and bitter disappointments. To Smalls, it was obvious that
the fight for freedom was far from over, and he had to stay in
the political arena to consolidate black gains.

In planning his political future, Smalls completely identified
himself with the Republican party. To him, this was "the party
of Lincoln which unshackled the necks of four millions human
beings." In the election campaigns in his constituency, Smalls
later recounted, he asked that "every colored man who has a
vote to cast would cast that vote for the regular republican party
and thus bury the democratic party so deep that there will not
be seen even a bubble coming from the spot where the burial
took place."[2] While blacks deserted the party when it was clear
the party had betrayed the cause for which it stood, Smalls remained steadfast until his death in 1915. As late as 1912 when the
two South Carolina Democratic senators opposed the confirmation of his re-appointment as the customs collector for Beaufort,
Smalls explained that he did not expect their support "being
myself what I have always been and expect to continue, a straightout republican." He continued, "I never can loose [sic] sight of
the fact that had it not been for the republican party, I never
would have been an office-holder of any kind—from 1862 to the
present."[3] He was a conspicuous participant in all Republican
state conventions, and was a delegate to several Republican national conventions.[4]

Smalls found political success by combining his appeal to Republicanism with a knowledge of the working of American poli-

[2] Smalls to Whitfield McKinlay, September 12, 1912, Letters to and from
Robert Smalls, Carter G. Woodson Papers, Library of Congress, Washington,
D.C.

[3] Smalls to Knute Nelson, U.S. Senator, August 22, 1912, Woodson Papers.

[4] Smalls was one of the alternate delegates to the National Republican
Convention at Chicago, May 20-21, 1868. He represented Beaufort district at
the Philadelphia Convention, June 5-6, 1872; the Cincinnati Convention,
June 14-16, 1876; and the Chicago Convention of June 3-4, 1884. He attended
subsequent conventions at St. Louis in 1896 and at Philadelphia in 1900.
Henry Wallace, "Letter Giving the Names of Negro Delegates to National
Republican Conventions," *Journal of Negro History*, VII (1922), 420-424;
Official Proceedings, Republican National Conventions, 1868-1872, 1876, 1880
(Minneapolis, 1903).

tics at the grass-roots level. He understood that the black majority
in his district would not necessarily insure his continued election
since many of the voters were obviously susceptible to the intimidation of the Democrats. Moreover, many of them did not understand the political implications of their newly acquired status
and had to be carefully guided by their leaders. Smalls understood this well and worked it to his political advantage. He
moved among his people explaining the meaning and power of
the vote. In 1903, he declined an invitation from a friend, Whitfield McKinlay, a black realtor in Washington, D.C., to come to
Washington because "we have a full county ticket in my county
to be voted for and arrangements for that have to be made" and
he was responsible for these. The black voters of Beaufort were
just as confused as others in the nation were about the persistent
wrangling in the Reconstruction years over corruption, exorbitant taxes, and the unresolved controversy over the lands seized
and sold under the direct tax laws. They threaded their way
through the confusion, however, by trusting the skipper of the
Planter to recognize the scoundrels. To his electorate, Smalls,
with a frequency bordering on vanity, would carry his "fine story"
which they never wearied of hearing. He exploited to his political
advantage their belief that he was the smartest black man in
South Carolina.[5]

Smalls' campaigns with a local band he had helped organize,
the Allen's Brass Band, and torchlight processions afforded his
constituents both entertainment and a vital sense of participation. Not to be outdone by prominent national Republicans,
Smalls built his own local political machine through the use of
the financial and educational institutions he had helped create
in the area. He kept his concern for the community well publicized by the local newspaper and even founded an organ of his
own, the *Standard*. He used Emancipation Memorial Day to enhance his political prestige. So effective was Smalls' local machine
that the Beaufort *Palmetto Post* complained that the free ballot
was a sham in the county. "Is it not common for the preachers

5 Smalls to McKinlay, October 22, 1902, Woodson Papers; also Rose, *Rehearsal*, 395-396.

to threat [sic] excommunication unless Bob Smalls' ticket is voted for?" the paper asked. "Is it not the practice for the women to vow abandonment from bed and board unless Smalls [receives a majority?]" Neighbors were threatened with assassination, by conjurer's spells, and by witchcraft unless they voted for Smalls, the paper alleged.[6]

Smalls' enormous property holdings in the county also became a political asset, especially after he won the case, De Treville vs. Smalls, in which the former tried to get back the Prince Street house Smalls had bought at government auction. This, in fact, became a test case for many blacks who owned land and other property on the islands and since many remained concerned about their property rights during Reconstruction, Smalls became their guide and leader on this important subject.[7]

Smalls' kind gesture toward the family of his former owner who had come to want in the new order redounded to his political advantage among the white inhabitants of the county. In the Reconstruction years, because of a loyalty to the McKees he had cultivated since slavery days, Smalls used his position to get employment for members of his former master's family and helped appoint one to the Naval Academy. He gave "substantial aid to the widow and children of his late master and to many white citizens of the town who have returned there since the war," a member of the McKee family recalled in 1877. By these various acts, one white paper commented, Smalls showed that, "while he has gone astray politically, he has a better heart than all the white scalawags and carpetbaggers of the South put together." Seeing the futility of putting up a white candidate in black-controlled Beaufort County during Reconstruction, the whites who cared to vote delivered the ballots to Robert Smalls. "The kindness of Smalls seems to have made a profound impression in his favor," the *News and Courier* observed on Smalls'

<hr>

[6] *Palmetto Post,* November 2, 1885; outside Charleston, Beaufort had more Republican newspapers than any county in the state. See Robert N. Woody, "Republican Newspapers in South Carolina," *Southern Sketches,* ed. J. D. Aggleston, Series 1, No. 16 (Charlottesville, Virginia, 1936), 20.

[7] Beaufort *Tribune,* November 3, January 6, 1875; Beaufort *Republican* June 27, 1872.

apparent popularity with the white people of Beaufort.[8] In fact, many white inhabitants of Beaufort regarded Smalls as the only one in the county who could maintain order and peace among his black constituents.

Historian Willie Lee Rose later attributed the continued electoral success of Robert Smalls to the fact that there was no other qualified person to challenge him. According to Mrs. Rose, the one man "who might have challenged Robert Smalls successfully, the most popular of the evangels with the Sea Islanders, had been Mansfield French. The minister, however, had returned North in 1872." Actually, however, French would have found it nearly impossible to oppose Robert Smalls successfully. The black people of Beaufort clearly had more confidence in black than in white leaders. As early as 1867, Laura Towne reported that at a meeting of blacks at which a few whites were present, one man rose to say he "wanted no white man in their platform." Though he was talked down by his more generous fellows, some of whom maintained that, if their skin is white, they may yet have principle,[9] there is no doubt that the blacks of Beaufort were more disposed to accept the leadership of their own people who were likely to win power. It must have been thrilling to them to have a leader like Smalls who could speak to them in their Gullah dialect, a corruption of the English language with many words of West African origin, a powerful man who was known to the editor of the *News and Courier* as "King of Beaufort County."[10]

Thus combining popularity and racial pride with appeals to Republicanism as the custodian of the rights of the freedmen, Smalls swept the polls at election after election in the Reconstruction years.

Election to the first General Assembly to gather under the new constitution was held between April 14 and 16, 1868. As was to

[8] W. E. McKee to Governor Wade Hampton, Hampton Papers. Beaufort *Tribune*, June 28, 1875; Charleston *News and Courier*, December 4, 1877. The *Tribune* blamed disturbance during an election campaign in 1876 on the absence of Robert Smalls, "the one man that could have controlled the rioters." Beaufort *Tribune*, November 1, 1876.

[9] Rose, *Rehearsal*, 393; Holland, *Towne Letters and Diary*, 182.

[10] Beaufort *Tribune*, May 12, 1875, quoting the Charleston *News and Courier*.

be expected, it was conducted in the face of great hostility from the conservative press and whites. As late as September 1868, a radical observer from Washington, John M. Morris, reported widespread intimidation and threats against blacks. They were "daily shot dead or wounded," he observed, and "nobody is convicted because no adequate testimony is found or the magistrates don't prosecute." He also noted, however, that the blacks were "shrewd though politically uneducated and lacking in experience and sagacity."[11] Thus, despite the hostile situation, the election was a huge success for the freedmen, who elected eighty-seven blacks as against forty whites.

On July 9, 1868, officers of the newly elected South Carolina government gathered at Janney's Hall in Columbia to take the oath of office that would release to them the keys to power. The new governor was Robert Kingston Scott, a heavily-mustachioed former Union general, and in popular parlance, a "carpetbagger," since he was among those who had recently come from the North supposedly to fill their bags with the riches of the South and head back North. The lieutenant governor was a native South Carolina white, Lamuel Boozer, a so-called "scalawag," a group former Confederates considered so mean and low as to betray the South by cooperating with carpetbaggers and Negroes during Reconstruction. Indicative of the new order, the secretary of state was Francis L. Cardozo, the prominent black spokesman in the late convention. Members of the new General Assembly followed in a procession, among them Robert Smalls, who had been elected to represent Beaufort County.

The business of the new government was to implement the new constitution. With black leaders conspicuously prominent, the legislature set out to revamp and strengthen the local government structures, revise the penal code, reverse the state's regressive tax system, which had spared the rich and soaked the poor, by shifting the burden of taxation from mercantile to landed property, and act upon the homestead provisions of the

[11] Cited by Jack B. Scroggs, "Southern Reconstruction: A Radical View," *Journal of Southern History* (November 1958).

new constitution. Smalls, an adroit politician, tried to relate all these issues to the needs of his constituents.

Most of his early legislative endeavors were calculated to help his constituents and thus enhance his political image. On July 21, 1868, he successfully introduced a resolution to transfer the county seat of Beaufort County from Gillisonville to his native Beaufort. Later, he introduced another resolution to establish a new election precinct in Beaufort. He was equally concerned with the serious state of disrepair of Beaufort's county jail and court house and got the legislature to authorize the levying of a special tax for the repairs of these public buildings. Apparently concerned about lack of cooperation between the Beaufort town council, still under the control of the former ruling class, and the new county government, Smalls called upon the General Assembly to appoint a commission to inquire into the attitude of the council, and served on the commission himself. In a subsequent report submitted to the Assembly, Smalls indicated how the situation was hampering the development of the area, and later worked to reconcile the two factions through mediation.

One obstacle to the development of Beaufort County was the inadequacy of the taxable resources in the area. Under the direct tax laws passed during the Civil War by which abandoned land could be sold for delinquent taxes, the whole parish of St. Helena had been sold, about 1500 pieces of property varying in size from five to one hundred and sixty acres, and one hundred town lots in Beaufort were held by the Federal Government. Besides, this valuable property was fast going into decay through neglect. To relieve the tax burden on the remaining taxable assets of his people, Smalls introduced a resolution for the Assembly to request the Congress to take appropriate action as would place "said property before the people of the said county of Beaufort for sale." He urged speedy action on the proposal, but failed to get it passed. He would try again as a state senator in 1872, and this would be one of the issues he would successfully fight for as a congressman in 1875.[12]

12 *Journal of the House of Representatives of the State of South Carolina Special and Regular Sessions,* 1868 (Columbia, S.C., 1869), 103, 119, 437; 388, 403, 641; also *House Journal,* Regular Session, 1869, 72, 78, 182.

Smalls was equally concerned with providing adequate transportation necessary for economic development in the Sea Islands. A projected railroad to connect Port Royal and Beaufort to Yemassee Junction, to be built by the Port Royal Railroad Company, chartered in 1857, had not succeeded by 1870. In that year, Smalls sought and obtained a franchise from the state legislature for the Beaufort Railroad Company, in which he himself apparently had a vested interest, which was then charged with the responsibility of building the road. By 1873 the road was completed, and, apart from providing needed transportation, it offered employment opportunities for numerous black families.[13]

Smalls did not allow himself to be bogged down with parochial but politically advantageous issues, however. The overall interests of his race were even more important than the specific problems of his district. Black political power in South Carolina, at least numerically speaking, had not been followed by social and economic equality, and Smalls was determined to secure these for the freedmen.

In April 1866, Congress, under the control of radical Republicans, had passed, over President Andrew Johnson's vetoes, a Civil Rights Act, and the Fourteenth Amendment had been ratified. The former extended citizenship to all Americans irrespective of their color and gave to each citizen the right to make contracts, sue, and hold real and personal property. The latter defined citizenship and enjoined the several states from abridging or violating the rights of citizens to life, liberty, property, and equal protection of the laws. Despite these proclamations, however, the hostility of whites in South Carolina, as indeed in the entire South, had made both measures virtually dead letters on the statute books. By 1867, the Ku Klux Klan, organized by young Tennesseans late in 1865 as a frolicking secret lodge and describing itself as an Invisible Empire dedicated to "chivalry, humanity, mercy, and patriotism," had spread to South Carolina and found new targets in black people whose increasing political and social activities constituted an affront to Southern patriotism! Soon to

---

[13] *House Journal,* Regular Session, 1869, 433-436; also George Brown Tindall, *South Carolina Negroes, 1877-1900* (Baton Rouge, 1966), 128-129.

be joined by similarly motivated groups pledged to maintain the old order, the Klan flogged, intimidated, maimed, hanged, and murdered blacks, not only for actual attacks and crimes against whites, but for all sorts of trivial and imagined offenses. "Towards the freedmen," a Freedmen Bureau agent at Greenville Court House, South Carolina, Major A. E. Niles, observed, "there is much bad feelings, [and] but for the presence of the garrison, I can hardly see how he would manage to live. The men that understand the freedmen to have, or that they are entitled to any more rights than a horse are exceptions to the general rule." A report submitted by John Harris, a special Republican agent to the state during preparation for the 1868 presidential election, was no less shocking. Black people, he observed, were shot dead daily and Democrats were openly proclaiming that no black man would be allowed to approach the polls. Equally concerned was Governor Robert Scott who warned that "the rebels did not misrepresent the fact when they said they were not whipped but only overpowered." In 1868, three members of the General Assembly and one member of the late constitutional convention were reported murdered.[14]

Allowing for possible exaggerations, these reports were too numerous to be mere figments of Radical imagination played up for political advantage. William A. Dunning, a generally proSouthern historian, concluded that "the moral suasion to which the leaders of the Klan would limit the movement against the Radicals never ceased to be supplemented by the merciless physical suasion in which rested the confidence of the rank and file." All evidence indicated that the Civil Rights Bill had not been properly enforced.[15]

In 1869, Robert Smalls called for the use of force, if necessary, to implement the provisions of the Civil Rights Bill of the United States Congress, but had little support in the House. In the next Session of the Legislature he introduced a bill to enforce by all

[14] A. E. Niles to Major H. W. Smith, May 2, 1866, cited by John Carpenter, "Atrocities in the Reconstruction Period," *Journal of Negro History* (April 1962); Robert Woody and Francis Simkins, *South Carolina During Reconstruction* (Chapel Hill, N.C., 1932), 446-447.

[15] Dunning, *Reconstruction*, 123.

means possible "the Civil Rights Bill of the United States Congress and secure to the people a republican government in this state." The bill was read and referred to the Committee on the Judiciary and died there.[16]

Meanwhile in Washington, Congress sought to strengthen the Reconstruction Acts by passing the Fifteenth Amendment which declared that the right to vote "shall not be denied . . . on account of race, color, or previous condition of servitude." Black leaders hailed it as ushering in the dawn of a new day. "I seem to myself," said Frederick Douglass, still the undisputed leader of black people, "to be living in a new world. The sun does not shine as it used. . . ." Even Wendell Phillips, the old abolitionist, was overwhelmed. "Slavery is dead," he declared. "We have not only abolished slavery, but we have abolished the Negro. We have actually washed color out of the constitution."

The champion of vigorous enforcement of the Civil Rights Act and the Fourteenth Amendment in South Carolina, Robert Smalls, was no less impressed. By February 1870, thirty states in the Union, including South Carolina, had ratified the amendment, and Smalls felt this was occasion enough for jubilation. As an expression of gratitude and hope in the promises held forth by this important milestone in the civil rights struggle, Smalls, on February 2, 1870, introduced the following preamble and resolution:

> Whereas, thirty states of the American Union have ratified the fifteenth Amendment to the Constitution of the United States; and whereas, this action of the American people fixes our government firmly on the side of right, and makes it a beacon light to the nations of the earth, and our flag the emblem of liberty, and the aegis of every citizen beneath its fold throughout the length and breadth of our land and the world over, and whereas, it is eminently proper that this great event should be hailed with joy and thanksgiving; therefore:
>
> Be it resolved . . . that, as an expression of our deep sense of gratitude to the Almighty God for this victory of right, and in honor of this event, His Excellency, the Governor, be requested to set apart a day of Thanksgiving and prayer immediately after the official notice of the ratification has been promulgated.[17]

[16] *House Journal, Regular Session,* 1868, 205, 237, 241, 332; *House Journal, Regular Session, 1869,* 289.
[17] *Ibid.,* 413.

The resolution was adopted by both the House and Senate. This resolution of Smalls reads like an affirmation of faith and confidence in the justice of the American system. It indicates the abundant hope that the blacks had during the Reconstruction Era. Using the advantage of hindsight, we know that these hopes were disappointed. Seen in the context of such affirmations as that of Smalls, the tragedy involved in the change of fortunes in the late 1870's is painful to contemplate. The disappointment was the more bitter because the hopes had been so high. With much truth has one historian labelled the black man "the tragic figure of the Reconstruction Era."[18]

In the House, Smalls continued to show great interest in relief and educational matters. He successfully worked to extend the provisions of a bill which sought to relieve the heirs of Mrs. Georgiana Heyward, widow of a Civil War veteran, from double tax execution to cover all persons in the state. Vigorous enforcement of the homestead law passed by the late constitutional convention had been hampered by the attitude of white sheriffs and other officers who, in most cases, favored the creditors rather than the debtors. Smalls, with the support of colleagues, successfully introduced a bill to punish such officers as interferred with the homestead law. Equally important was his continued interest in education for the poor and needy in recognition of which Smalls was elected a member of the newly created Commission to Effect the Establishment of a System of Free Common Schools in the state.

Though Smalls utilized the opportunities offered by the economic dislocation following the Civil War to establish a secure economic base, he did not, contrary to the traditional stereotype of black politicians during Reconstruction, look upon political office as a means of preying on the public. He was for austerity in government spending and opposed to extravagance. He supported his House colleagues who successfully opposed a resolution to allow the speaker "in addition to his regular per diem, an extra compensation of (4) dollars per diem." He opposed the con-

18 Rembert W. Patrick, *The Reconstruction of the Nation* (New York 1967), 247.

tinued payment of per diem to any member of the legislature granted leave of absence on a plea of important business. When calling for the adjournment of the General Assembly in 1868, Smalls pleaded that no per diem should be paid to either members or employees of the legislature during the period of adjournment. In the 1869 session of the House, Smalls also called for the regulation of the fees of probate judges, clerks of the courts, trial justices, justices of the peace, and other officers. His increasing concern with maladministration, corruption, and extravagance in government spending would become more evident in the 1870's, later to be considered the years of "good stealing" in South Carolina.[19]

A promising new sphere of usefulness opened for Robert Smalls in 1870 when he was elected to fill a vacancy in the Senate occasioned by the resignation of J. J. Wright of Beaufort County. He had been nominated by a rump convention which met in his house and had a "splendid run" in the election, beating his opponent by more than 4000 votes.[20]

Along with Smalls, twelve other new senators were chosen in an election which D. T. Corbin, Acting Lieutenant Governor and President pro tempore of the senate, described as "a most bitter and acrimonious campaign, in which the feelings of our constituents and fellow-citizens have been wrought up to the highest pitch." In an atmosphere fraught with suspicion and hysteria aggravated by mounting hostility between the races, the legislators had to address themselves to the economic, social, and political problems of the state, which called for wisdom, caution, and experience. In November 1870, Governor Scott put on a brave front in his address to the Assembly and spoke of "gratifying evidence of material progress and improvement surrounding us, and the general indications of the prevalence of peace and harmony within the state." Gratification soon turned to despair, however, and optimism gave place to concern. "Insecurity of life and property prevailed in several counties." Charges of corruption, extravagance, and incompetence on the part of the ad-

---

[19] *House Journal,* Regular Session, 1868 and 1869, 76, 179, 189; 508.
[20] Beaufort *Republican,* September 23 and October 7, 1870.

ministration were alleged, believed, and heralded throughout the country. The Ku Klux Klan raids reached a peak of barbarity to the extent that by 1871 the writ of habeas corpus was suspended and the Federal troops called in. Public confidence in the state government was nearly destroyed. A change of tone was evident in the governor's speech to the legislature on November 28, 1871. He reported a critical financial situation in the state with the debt rising from $5,375,208.98 in 1870 to $22 million. The organized murder of blacks by whites begun in 1865, he continued, had culminated in the Klan raids "which differed in its destructiveness from actual war only in this, that *the killed and wounded were all on one side*." He equated the raids with disloyalty to the government since he could not regard "men loyal to the government who set its laws at defiance, and use every means in their power to destroy its very existence." He called upon the members to "legislate in the interest of the whole people of the state," and prove to the country at large that "Republicanism and good government in South Carolina are not, as is falsely alleged, inconsistent with each other." With these sentiments the legislators concurred when they resolved unanimously to accept the address.[21]

Robert Smalls was designated by his fellow senators to play a leading role in this enormous task. In the 1871-72 session of the senate, Smalls was appointed a member of important committees: mining and mines, county offices and officers, and finance. As before, however, Smalls' foremost concern was the deteriorating situation in his home county.

Reports indicated that, despite earlier attempts by Smalls and others in the previous years to improve them, the economic conditions of Beaufort, and indeed of the Sea Islands, remained largely far from satisfactory in the 1870's. Edisto Island lands that had ranged in value from seventy-five dollars to a hundred dollars an acre at the end of the war had gone down to less than thirty dollars by 1867, and by 1873 the value of plantation lands around Beaufort was only six or seven dollars. The amount of land under cultivation in the county had fallen from 259,543 in

[21] *Journal of the Senate of the General Assembly of the State of South Carolina*, Regular Session, 1870 and 1871, 6, 41; 8-48.

1860 to 150,000 acres in 1870. "Let us glance at the promises and anticipations of four years ago, and then look to see how they have been fulfilled," James Thompson, former Philadelphia newspaperman and now editor of the Beaufort *Republican,* announced as he took stock in 1872. He recalled that in 1868, the young Republican Party had resolved "upon a vigorous campaign against the abuses fostered by the pro-slavery spirit. . . . It determined upon an honest, economical but liberal government of the people by the people." Thompson felt that the party had not achieved any of these goals, and that Port Royal freedmen were the greatest victim of this failure. To a Springfield (Philadelphia) *Republican* correspondent, everything in Beaufort was "flavored with decay." The houses were unkept, indicating "only too sadly the prosperity that has fled from their owners." Neither the natural beauty of the area nor the singing of mockingbirds could remove the air of desertion that permeated the town. "Utter stagnation," the correspondent concluded, seemed to be the "only fate in store for it." Even Laura Towne was embarrassed by the lack of improvement in the area. "Sometimes it seems like work thrown away, especially just after reading in the newspapers and seeing the estimation in which our state is held by the rest of the world, and not undeservedly," she wrote to a Northern supporter of her work.[22]

Generally, this situation was attributed to the ignorance and inability of the blacks and their leaders. To the former wartime Gideonite, Edward King, the blacks were "too busy with politics to work." In Beaufort, King noted, they "monopolize everything," and were "in possession of a great deal" that they were unable to use. King, who had loved the blacks when he was their teacher and superior, was now worried that "the vassals" (blacks) of the community "have become lords, and dispose of the present and pledge the future resources of the state." James S. Pike, a Radical journalist who had advocated Negro suffrage in 1865 but had become a bitter opponent of the Radicals in Washington by 1872,

22 Beaufort *Republican,* November 16, 1871, May 23 and July 11, 1872, and December 26, 1873; Beaufort *Tribune,* February 24, 1875; Towne to Francis R. Cope, July 12, 1874, quoted by Rose, *Rehearsal,* 384; also Johnson, *A Social History of the Sea Islands,* 202-203.

was no less concerned with the new role of the enfranchised blacks. In a book published in 1873 in which he lampooned Radical Reconstruction in South Carolina, he reported that the state "lay prostrate in the dust, ruled over by this strange conglomerate, gathered from the ranks of its own servile population. It is the spectacle of a society suddenly turned bottom-side up." The new political role of black South Carolinians appeared to have been a matter of greater concern than the economic situation.[23]

Robert Smalls understood the situation and did his best to change it. The heart of the matter, as he saw it, was a need for his people to become land-owning farmers. Much of the fertile land in the area was in the hands of the Federal Government and his earlier attempts to get it back had met with no success. On February 9, 1872, Smalls again introduced in the Senate a concurrent resolution asking support for a bill to return to the people the land confiscated by the United States District Tax Commissioners between 1863 and 1866. "The longer occupation of these lands by the Federal Government," he argued, would "be a serious and insurmountable obstacle to the prosperity of the said county of Beaufort, inasmuch as no improvements not even repairs, are being, or will be made thereon, consequently, said property is rapidly deteriorating in value—many valuable houses having already fallen into ruins." He asked the legislature to instruct the South Carolina Senators and Representatives "to use their immediate and most earnest endeavors to secure the passage of said Bill or such other legislation" and thus relieve his people "from this incubus upon their prosperity." The resolution was passed and forwarded to the South Carolina congressional delegation. Action was delayed, however, until 1875, when Smalls himself, by then a member of the United States Congress, got the bill passed. Thus, through Smalls' efforts, the blacks of Beaufort were finally able to buy land at cheap prices. In 1877, the secretary of state for South Carolina reported that "a vast amount of marsh lands on the coast, particularly near Beaufort" was

[23] Edward King, *The Southern States of North America* (Glasgow and Edinburgh, 1875), 483; James S. Pike, *The Prostrate State: South Carolina Under Negro Government* (New York, 1874), 12.

increasing in value. By 1890, three-fourths of the land in Beaufort was owned by blacks.[24]

The black people of Beaufort also realized that social improvement would not come if they sat by idly expecting manna from the government. Smalls and other black leaders in the area realized the importance of self-help in initiating social change. During the Reconstruction period, they tried to form co-operatives for their own uplift. One such project was the Beaufort Manufacturing and Improvement Company. Alfred Williams, Robert Smalls, W. J. Whipper, J. Douglass Robertson, David Thomas, N. B. Myers, Francis E. Wilder, James Crofut, George Holmes, and other blacks formed this company "for the purpose of extracting and manufacturing oil from cotton seed, and other seeds or grain, and for the purpose of carrying on such other business connected therewith." The capital was to be one hundred thousand dollars each. The company could increase its capital stock to any amount not exceeding two hundred and fifty thousand dollars. It could build wharves to aid its business and could collect wharfage. It could also build roads provided that "the lines of said road, so far as it affects the town of Beaufort, shall be fixed and established by the Intendant Council thereof."[25]

Robert Smalls introduced a bill in the Senate to incorporate this company, and on March 9, 1872, it was approved. The company was to go into operation when "thirty thousand dollars of capital stock shall be paid, in gold or silver, or United States Treasury notes." Apparently, the company did not go into operation. Apart from financial difficulties, most of the prospective shareholders departed the state with the advent of Democratic rule in 1876. Smalls and his friends obviously hoped to make money, but the project also indicated their appreciation of the importance of self-help for economic improvement.

24 *Senate Journal,* Regular Session, 1871-72, 413-414; *Reports and Resolutions of the General Assembly of the State of South Carolina at the Regular Session, 1876-77* (Columbia, S.C., 1877), 352; *First Mohonk Conference on the Negro Question,* June 4, 5, 6 (Boston, 1890); also Rose, *Rehearsal,* 397.

25 *Acts and Resolutions of the General Assembly of the State of South Carolina Passed at the Regular Session of 1871-72* (Columbia, S.C., 1872), 113-115.

Smalls' interests in his Senate years included other issues which, though having direct bearing on his constituency, affected the whole state. The conduct of the mining companies engaged in the exploitation of the phosphate deposits in the coastal regions of the state had been a subject of great concern. In 1870, Charles U. Shephard, Jr., the state Inspector of Guano and Fertilizer, had called for control of the phosphate companies to help increase the state revenue. The Marine and River Phosphate Mining and Manufacturing Company, for example, was constantly defaulting in payment of royalties. State Senator D. T. Corbin, president of the company, refused to acknowledge the right of the state to pass supervisory laws and denied the Inspector the right to exercise authority delegated to him by the government. The state was thus clearly losing valuable assets to unscrupulous speculators.

Smalls took up the matter and introduced a strongly worded resolution in which he condemned the phosphate companies for their failure to make "just and full returns to the state auditor." He called upon the Senate to institute a committee of five to investigate and report on the returns of all companies engaged in mining in the navigable streams and rivers of the state, and to inquire into the right of the companies to be in operation. The findings of the committee showed that the state was losing from the enterprise, the Marine and River Phosphate Mining and Manufacturing Company paying only $1989 to the state. To stop this drain of revenue and better regulate the companies, Smalls called for the appointment of an Inspector of Phosphates whose duties should be defined by law and he aided in enforcing his decisions by the state courts. He suggested and won support for Otto Moses, whose report for 1872 showed an honest approach to the problem and goaded the government on to further action. By 1876, the state had gone a long way in regulating the companies, and state attorney general, James Connor, reported in that year the full collection of all royalties due the state from the mining companies.[26]

[26] Senate Journal, Regular Session, 1870 and 1871, 46; 195; Report of the State Inspector of Phosphates, Reports and Resolutions of the General Assembly of the State of South Carolina at the Regular Session of 1872-73 (Columbia, S.C., 1873), 716-720.

The proper exploitation of the phosphate beds was a godsend to black laborers as well as to the whites who organized the mining companies. Many a Port Royal black left his farm for his wife and children to cultivate while he went to the "rock," as the phosphate mines in the coastal counties were called, to get "cash money." "Our colored friends can look to the future with pleasure and know that they will not have to roam over the country next summer to look for work but will find it on Bull River at the Oak Point Mine," the *Republican* commented on the new opportunities opened to the Sea Islanders. Black labor was employed almost exclusively in the mines, especially after attempts to use Italian labor failed in the 1880's. In fact the editor believed the temporary threat posed by the latter "improved the character of Negro labor" by showing the blacks that the miners were "not alone dependent upon them for their labor." Although the majority of the blacks rarely made enough money to carry them through the year, there were some who prospered. At the close of Reconstruction, many two-story houses with porches, window panes, and a neat coat of paint had begun to appear in the area. "Poverty-stricken indeed was the man who did not have a sunday suit," one Northern visitor observed in 1878. By spearheading the fight for the regulation of the mining companies, Smalls had rendered yet another service to his community.[27]

In the Senate, Smalls continued his long-time fight to curb excesses in government spending, particularly those involving salaries of government and elected officers. As a member of the finance committee, he pushed through the senate a bill to fix the compensation and fees of solicitors in criminal cases. He called for the immediate discharge of all special and joint investigating committees appointed by the legislature on the completion of their duties. This had been a source of waste as members of such committees had continued to draw pay for work long completed.

Smalls' posture in this regard was supported by many of his black colleagues, and their action suggests that the much publicized view that all the black legislators were active participants

[27] Beaufort *Republican*, November 23, 1871; S. G. W. Benjamin, "The Sea Islands," *Harper's New Monthly Magazine*, LVII (1878), 839-861; Charleston *News and Courier*, March 1, 1884.

and promoters of the waste and extravagance of South Carolina's
Reconstruction government needs serious modification. No doubt
some of the black leaders partook in the sharing of the spoils,
but this was partly because their white mentors very often set a
bad example. "The colored members of the legislation [sic] took
bribes and did jobs because they look eagerly to see what to do
in their new circumstances, to their white brethren, and as they
saw, or were instructed so they did in imitation, and thought it
was the proper thing," one contemporary observed.[28]

Smalls' first term in the Senate expired in 1872, and he was up
for re-election. By this time, however, his political dominance in
the county was being challenged by W. J. Whipper, a Northern
black who had come South shortly after the war. A lawyer by
training, Whipper "combined with his extravagant and spend-
thrift habits . . . a good many qualities of generosity and good-
ness of heart." He identified himself with the "Reform" wing
of the Republican party, and attacked Smalls for his connection
with the existing Republican administration which was constantly
being charged with extravagance and corruption. The reform
case was eloquently pleaded by the Beaufort *Tribune*.[29]

Apparently afraid that the "defectors" were winning many con-
verts, Smalls used his chairmanship of the Beaufort County Republican party to good advantage. Without giving public notice,
he summoned the "faithful" to a meeting in his house where he
hand-picked delegates to the state convention meeting in Columbia to choose a complete slate of candidates and ratify the nomination of Grant for President. As one would expect, the
Beaufort delegation was pledged to the success of its boss, Robert
Smalls, in the impending election.[30]

With his nomination secured, Smalls opened a vigorous campaign. Being himself increasingly concerned with the reputation
of the state Republican party, Smalls called for "a more careful

[28] Towne to Francis Cope, July 12, 1874, cited by Rose, *Rehearsal*, 384.
[29] This view of Whipper, who was to become a center of attention as one
of the supposedly corrupt judges elected by the legislature, was given by a
white townsman in 1882. Charleston *News and Courier*, January 12, 1882.
[30] Resolution of Beaufort Citizens, Legislative System, 1866-1877, Election
Miscellaneous, Beaufort County, South Carolina Archives, Columbia, South
Carolina. This was a resolution passed by the "Reformers."

scrutiny of the character of the state ticket." He constantly attacked Governor Scott for being soft on reform. Hopeful that Smalls might give in to the increasingly vituperative attack from the county press, the "reformers" announced that Smalls was considering resigning his chairmanship of the local Republican party, and paving the way for the election of Whipper. "My friends need have no fear of my resigning or surrendering to the enemy," Smalls struck back. "My guns are in position and will continue to pour hot shot into the ranks of traitors and adventurers." He warned the blacks against trusting "outsiders" who came to the area to exploit the people. At a meeting on St. Helena Island, Smalls was received "with great enthusiasm and his account of the political situation was listened to with attention." Later in the canvass, a rival newspaper noted that Smalls dealt his opponents "very heavy blows" and the people "manifested their confidence in him and their utter disregard of his enemies. They showed by the most unmistakable signs that their confidence in him was unshaken, and that the efforts of his enemies to produce the contrary result had proved futile." This was reflected in the number of votes cast for Smalls. "The countrymen could not resist an invitation to jump into Smalls' wagon and ride to the polls," the *Tribune* editorialized on the size of Smalls' majority. Another paper commented that the Sea Islanders were more interested in "Robert Smalls the man than in Robert Smalls the exponent of certain political issues." So impressive was Smalls' success and so devastating the blow he dealt his opponents that when Smalls left for the United States Congress in 1874, he chose his own successor to the Senate seat.[31]

Smalls' stand on the gubernatorial race between Franklin Moses and Reuben Tomlinson also merits some attention. The fight within the national Republican party which led to the nomination of Horace Greeley to run against President Grant in the 1872 presidential election also split the South Carolina Republicans. Reuben Tomlinson emerged as the leader of the reform group in South Carolina and was nominated for governor.

31 Beaufort *Republican,* August 22, 1872; *Ibid.,* May 30, August 1, September 26, October 10, 1872; Beaufort *Tribune,* May 19, 1875.

To run against him, the "Regular Republicans" nominated a "scalawag," Franklin Moses. From his critical stand on several issues during the previous administration, Smalls might have been expected to support Tomlinson. He had himself called for reform and for a moment thought of forming a third party "based on intelligence and integrity" in the Sea Islands, but he supported Moses.

Though critical of the Regular Republican party, Smalls still identified it as the "party of Lincoln," and this to him was "above all other considerations." He attended the National Republican Convention which re-nominated Grant. On the local level, he worked to defeat the reform group. As the greatest political force in the Sea Islands, he swung the black vote for the regulars, and opposed Tomlinson with warnings that the freedmen "could not trust outsiders, that they should vote for none but Southern men." The appeal worked, and Reuben Tomlinson, who had worked with much credit and universal acclaim among the Sea Islanders, lost the race, receiving a meager vote of 1445 to 4995 for Moses, in Beaufort County. Even in the Brick Church precinct, the immediate vicinity of his old headquarters as General Superintendent under Saxton, Tomlinson received 62 votes to 631 for Moses. On breaking down the votes, editor Thompson of the *Republican* found that they were divided between the two candidates largely on the basis of color, with the white people voting for Tomlinson, and the black voters, following Smalls, voting for Moses.[32]

The reasons why Robert Smalls, who had been so vocal for reform, preferred F. J. Moses, a blatant swindler, to Reuben Tomlinson, conspicuous for his attempts to bring the benefits of education to Smalls' people, merit some attention. Actually, the two candidates were not so far apart on their record on honesty. Because of his involvement with the transactions of the Columbia and Greenville Railroad, to be discussed later, Tomlinson was scarcely a paragon of virtue in the public eye. One of the most

[32] Charleston *News and Courier*, April 6, November 13, 1871, describes Small's attempt at forming a third party. Woody and Simkins, *South Carolina During Reconstruction*, 446-467, list Smalls as a bolter from the regulars; Beaufort *Republican*, July 11, October 24, 1872.

outstanding grafts of the period in South Carolina involved this railroad, and Tomlinson was the treasurer of the company and also the state attorney general when the crucial transactions were made. Also, Tomlinson was 'frequently charged with bribery, especially when he wanted the legislature to grant franchises to phosphate companies he was promoting. To many people, the contest was not really between "the corrupt Moses" and the honest Tomlinson. Indeed, commented one paper, "the good people simply look upon the entire contest as a struggle between thieves and plunderers, and have no preference between the combatants."[33]

For Smalls, however, the most probable motive was political expediency. As noted earlier, he was being opposed for the Senate in the same election by Whipper, a Northern black. In this situation, the magic wand of race as a campaign appeal could no longer work. Moreover, Whipper was exploiting Smalls' lack of formal education and alleged participation in the corruption of the Regulars. Smalls apparently feared that supporting Tomlinson might seriously jeopardize his chances of success against Whipper. Thus, faced with choosing between support for a somewhat questionable candidate and a cause which would better protect his own political future, Smalls elected to oppose Tomlinson. Whipper was probably not a real threat to Smalls but politicians rarely feel secure in election years.[34]

By November 1872, when the new session of the Legislature opened, a calmer atmosphere prevailed in the state. The Ku Klux Klan raids had been stopped, and the president of the Senate announced the coming of a new "peace and sense of security" and a "better state of feeling . . . especially between the two races or classes composing, in the main, the two political parties." In his inaugural, Governor Moses was equally certain that "peace and good order now prevail everywhere within the state, which

[33] Charleston *News and Courier,* September 26, 1872, quoting the *Edgefield Advertiser;* Reynolds, *Reconstruction in South Carolina,* 126 233, Simkins and Woody, *South Carolina During Reconstruction,* 204-206, describe the contest.
[34] Beaufort *Republican,* August 22, September 26, 1872.

seem to be accompanied by a returning sense of justice, and by a broader spirit of toleration in the hitherto ruling classes."[35]

In this session, Robert Smalls continued to serve on important committees: Claims, Finance, Mines and Mining, Penitentiary, Contingent Accounts, and most importantly, in the light of future events, he served as the chairman of the Committee on Printing. In 1874, he was elected a regent of the State Lunatic Asylum. By the latter part of that year, Smalls had in fact gained a commanding voice in the Senate, and dictated, as it were, the appointment of the chairmen of various important committees.[36]

As before, Smalls continued to act as the watchdog for the interests of his constituency. To further improve transportation in the area, he obtained authorization for William Kressel and John Eider Ohland to build docks and wharves in the area. He pushed through bills to incorporate the Port Royal Dock and Transportation Warehouse and Banking Company, and also the Railroad Rolling Stock Manufacturing Company of Port Royal. He was equally interested in getting acts of incorporation for the various self-help projects which sprang up in the area, including the Longshoremen's Protective Association of Port Royal, the Port Royal Hydraulic Cotton Press Company of Beaufort County, and the Ladies' Branch Society of St. Helena Island. He got the Legislature to appoint an Inspector of Timber and Lumber for Port Royal harbor. It would appear that many of these industrial projects did not last very long. At the end of Reconstruction, Beaufort, and indeed the Sea Island area, showed a very meager business development in comparison with other parts of the state. In 1878, there was only one small black store in the town of Beaufort, one or two black tailors, a harnessmaker, and several black carpenters and tradesmen.[37]

The 1870's was a period when corruption and extravagance in South Carolina reached their high point, and Smalls' stand on

[35] *Journal of the Senate of the General Assembly of the State of South Carolina, Regular Session, 1872-73* (Columbia, S.C., 1873), 7, 45.

[36] *Journal of the Senate of the General Assembly of the State of South Carolina, Regular Session, 1874-75* (Columbia, S.C., 1875), 46-60.

[37] *Ibid.*, 13-14; *Journal of the Senate of the State of South Carolina for the Regular Session of 1872-74* (Columbia, S.C., 1874), 525-526; *Senate Journal,* Regular Session, 1874-75, 15-40.

such issues should be noted. During these years, and especially under the governorship of Franklin Moses from 1872 to 1874, "the sorely tried commonwealth literally fell among thieves," to quote a later Southern historian. "About the corpse of the dead state, a flock of ghouls gathered." The pages of the *Republican* were filled with "every act of fraud, every waste of means, every increase in debt, every job of extravagance and knavery." In 1873, the embittered Republican James Pike denounced in scornful language the corruption of the South Carolina Legislature in The *Prostrate State*. South Carolina was indeed acting out its part in the national drama.[38]

White supremacists as well as some early historians were unanimous in blaming the corruption on blacks, along with the "scalawags" and "carpetbaggers." A careful examination of the facts, and especially those relating to Robert Smalls, however, would show that far from being active participants, some of the black leaders tried to check the corruption. A contemporary black legislator had in fact cautioned against generalizing about corruption among the blacks. The white opposition "gave them [the blacks] no credit for their honest efforts at reform, but attributed base and corrupt motives to the best intentioned measures, and indulged in indiscriminate and insulting taunts and ridicule . . . confounding the pure and the corrupt, the honest and the dishonest, the statesman and the demagogue, and pouring obliquy [sic] on all alike," he alleged.[39]

In 1871, the discouraged Rufus Saxton, now living in the North, wrote to Robert Smalls for an explanation of the situation in the state. In his letter, Saxton recalled the emotions of the black soldiers and their friends at the news of the Emancipation Proclamation, and his admonition to the freedmen to be "honest, industrious, temperate, true and pure." General Saxton had "rejoiced when the right of suffrage came and sorrowed

38 E. C. McCants, *History Stories and Legends of South Carolina* (Texas, 1927), 389; Beaufort *Republican,* July 11, May 23, 1872. For a brief discussion of the national situation see Richard Hofstadter, "The Spoilsmen: An Age of Cynicism," *American Political Traditions and the Men Who made Them* (New York, 1961), 164-185.

39 See "A Southern Visit," *The Friend* (Philadelphia), XLIX (March 11, 1876), 237.

when it was told that some had sold this precious birthright for
a miserable mess of pottage." Though he did not believe all he
heard, he feared that "where there is so much smoke there must
be some fire." The last part of the letter referred to Smalls personally. In scolding but fatherly language, General Saxton reminded Smalls of his heroic exploits with the *Planter*. "The ship
of state of South Carolina," he reminded the pilot hero, "is now
in stormy waters. The rocks and shoals, torpedoes and hostile
guns are ignorance, immorality, dishonesty, and corruption in
high places. The beacon lights ahead are honesty, intelligence,
the school house and the church." He admonished Smalls to keep
the helm of the ship of state "steady toward these and soon the
ship shall glide gently by the breakers into the peaceful waters
of freedom."[40]

Smalls was extremely touched, and used the occasion of the
Emancipation Day celebration in 1871 to read the letter to his
constituents. Following a parade of militiamen, he dismounted
from his horse, climbed to the speaker's stand, and "solemnly,"
reported the *Republican,* read Saxton's letter. Solemnly, he
pledged to fight for reforms, indicating that "the reputation I
gained in bringing out the *Planter* I do not intend to sully by my
actions as a member of the state legislature." He continued:

> As well as I knew the beacon lights in the time of the *Planter,* I
> know the beacon lights now, and the channel that leads to honesty,
> virtue, purity and intelligence, and I trust that I may ever be found
> working with those who are anxious to guide the ship of state of
> South Carolina from the dark and troubled waters in which she is
> now, safe past the rocks, torpedos and hostile guns of ignorance, im-
> morality and dishonesty in high places to the calm and placid waters
> of that harbor where religious, social, moral and political purity
> reign supreme.[41]

He promised that his voice would be heard assisting in the conviction of those whom he believed to be dishonest. Amid great
temptations, Smalls tried to live up to this pledge.

Though the Democrats often associated Smalls with the cor-

[40] Rufus Saxton to Robert Smalls, Beaufort *Republican,* January 4, 1872.
[41] *Ibid.*

rupt element in the Republican party, available evidence does not bear this out and in fact suggests the contrary. In the Senate, Smalls worked constantly against extravagance and corruption in government. He successfully introduced a bill to protect the state against the fraudulent tender of bills of the bank of the state in payment of taxes, and supported proposals for protecting merchants, factors, and common carriers against exploitation. He asked and got the Senate to pass a bill requiring the prompt return of reports of the financial situation in their offices by the comptroller general and state and county officers. Under this bill, Smalls subsequently spearheaded the prosecution of two county treasurers.[42]

One of the most notorious grafts of the period involved the Sinking Fund Commission, organized in 1870 under the chairmanship of Governor Scott to sell "unproductive property of the state." Among the transactions of the Commission was the sale of the 21,698 shares of stock of the Greenville and Columbia Railroad to New York syndicates at $2.75 per share. The state had paid $20 per share for the property and thereby lost over three hundred and eighty thousand dollars. So devastating was the blow dealt the economy that the Senate appointed a committee under Smalls' chairmanship to investigate the handling of the transactions.

The investigation revealed a corrupt bargain between the parties involved. Smalls called upon the Legislature to institute legal proceedings against the culprits. This started promptly, but proved generally unsuccessful because many of them left the state following the election of 1876.[43]

The stigma of corruption fastened to the Republican party during the governorship of Franklin Moses became a matter of great concern to the state's Republican leadership, including Smalls. At the state convention of 1874, presided over by Smalls, the Republicans reacted and nominated Daniel Chamberlain, a

[42] *Senate Journal,* **Regular Session,** 1874-75, **656, 669;** also 1872-73, 495, 426, 698; *1873-74,* 30, 31.

[43] *Report and Resolutions of the General Assembly of the State of South Carolina, 1873-74* (Columbia, S. C., 1874), 753-787; *Senate Journal,* Regular Session 1873-74, 271.

white Northern-born graduate of Harvard and Yale Law School who had come South during the war, as their gubernatorial candidate and drew up a platform dedicated to reform and promised to make "the practice and enforcement of economy and honesty" the keynote of the next Republican administration. They also promised to "purify" the administrative system and thereby cleanse their party of its unfortunate reputation for corruption and misrule. Smalls campaigned actively for Chamberlain and the reform platform, and delivered the votes of the Sea Islanders to the party. As governor, Chamberlain was both hardworking and honest.[44]

Smalls did not go unscathed during these years, however. So deeply was he involved with Republican politics that it was very easy to connect him in some way with the corruption and dishonesty of Republican rule in South Carolina. Thus, when the Democrats came into power in 1876, Smalls was one of the subjects of the investigations and prosecutions carried out by the "redeemer government" in 1876 and 1877.

It was alleged that, while he was chairman of the committee on printing, Smalls had counseled Josephus Woodruff, Clerk of the Senate, and A. O. Jones, Clerk of the House, to commit a breach of trust with fradulent intention by certifying that a Senate printing claim for $25,000 had been passed and approved by the Assembly. He was alleged to have received $5000 from the transaction. He was indicted, tried and convicted, and sent to serve a three-year term in the state penitentiary.

An examination of the character of the prosecution witness, the evidence on which the case was built, and the general procedure of the case, leaves the distinct impression that the conviction of Robert Smalls was a miscarriage of justice and motivated by political vendetta.

Before the trial came up, there was general excitement and enthusiasm about Smalls' impending conviction. The "boat thief" of the Civil War years, as he was known to the Confederates, was now a target whose reputation was delivered to Democratic jour-

[44] Beaufort *Republican*, November 1, 1873; Charleston *News and Courier*, August 23 and September 5, 1874.

nalists, to whom taking pot shot at this "irresponsible and corrupt Negro" was an exhilarating sport. They pronounced him guilty even before the actual trial, and were extremely delighted about THE DOWNFALL OF SMALLS. To the *News Courier* Smalls' had already become the "culprit Congressman." (Before the trial came up Smalls was in the Congress). In this atmosphere, there was little hope of a fair trial for Smalls in the state. For, as Smalls' attorney, Judge Carpenter, admitted while addressing the court, "it is almost impossible to keep political feelings out of the courtroom." The judge was even threatened for daring to defend Smalls. "You must be very fond of being killed," a certain man told the judge. "You were killed first politically, then judicially, and now you are killing yourself professionally in defending these criminals." In this atmosphere the verdict of guilty was a foregone conclusion.[45]

The case against Robert Smalls rested on the evidence of Josephus Woodruff, who had himself confessed to robbing the state of over $250,000 and had run away, but had been brought back from Pennsylvania after he had entered into a deal with South Carolina to surrender part of his loot and property and thus buy "immunity" and become a state witness. Evidence from such a man could hardly be trusted, according to Smalls' attorney, because Woodruff had not only surrendered "his property but also surrendered himself to the attorney general to testify when he was required, and against whosoever required." At the trial, "the self-confessed thief," as Smalls later described him, admitted that he had been granted immunity from trial because he had promised the prosecution to testify against Smalls. Smalls' other lawyer, Judge Melton, described Woodruff as "a systematic, constitutional, hereditary wool-dyed liar, who was purchasing immunity by testifying in these cases." Indeed, one cannot escape the impression that Woodruff was merely working for the Democratic party in his own best interest.[46]

Woodruff's evidence was no more convincing than his person.

45 Charleston *News and Courier*, November 12, 1877.

46 Charleston *News and Courier*, November 12, 1877; *Journal of the Constitutional Convention of the State of South Carolina, 1895* (Columbia, S.C., 1895), 475.

Reading from his "little black book shorthand notes that no one else could read," he testified that he credited to the account of Smalls in the Banking and Trust Company of the state a check dated January 18, 1873 in the sum of $5000. This, Smalls indicated later, was designed to square with the fact that he had deposited an identical amount on that day and Woodruff knew it. When examined, the records showed that the check which Smalls deposited was dated 19 January. The Democrats claimed that this was simply a clerical error. In this situation, it was appropriate to call in the cashier of the bank, one Jacobs, to testify. But Jacobs himself had fled the state after being charged four times with perjury. In his absence, a man named Zeeley brought in a little slip of paper written in pencil, which he claimed to be Jacob's handwriting, and his evidence was accepted as corroborating that of Woodruff.

Equally suspect was Woodruff's evidence that he had arranged with Smalls to push through the proposal in the Senate on January 15, 1873, exactly half a month after the bill had in fact been passed. How then could Woodruff have bribed Smalls to do what had in fact been done? So inconclusive, indeed, was Woodruff's evidence and so unproven his charges, that, when balanced against Smalls' proven honesty in so many other matters, the weight of credibility clearly rests with Smalls' own version that this was a "trumped-up charge against me for the purpose of making me resign."

When Smalls was arrested in 1876, Laura Towne noted that the Democrats had "two objects in this. One is to prevent his taking his seat in the approaching congress, and the other to bring odium upon him and give his opponent in the contested seat a better chance." Between the arrest and the trials, it was widely alleged that the prosecutions and trials were in fact designed to induce certain prominent Republicans who still held office to resign. Though the Charleston *News and Courier* dismissed the allegation as a "mere invention of Senator Patterson, one of the accused," there was much logic in this line of reasoning.[47]

[47] Holland, *Towne Letters and Diary,* 279; Charleston *News and Courier,* August 8, 1877.

Smalls later testified that, while he was detained in Columbia pending the trial, two important people visited him. The first was John Cochrane, Chairman of the Investigation Committee, and, according to Smalls, the conversation went as follows:

> "Smalls, you must resign."
> "Resign what?" Smalls asked.
> "Resign your seat in Congress."
> "What," fumed Smalls, "the seat the people elected me to?"
> "Yes, you had better resign, because if you don't they are going to convict you."
> "I don't believe that, Sir," Smalls replied, "I am innocent and they cannot do it."
> "Well," said Mr. Cochrane, "bear in mind that these men have the court, they have got the jury, and an indictment is a conviction."[48]

Next came "another gentleman," Mr. Drayton, a newspaper editor from Aiken County. He entreated Smalls "to get out of the way," pleading that "Governor Hampton says he doesn't want to injure you. We want this government, and we must have it." He promised Smalls that he would be paid $10,000 for his two years' salary in the Congress. Smalls was indignant. "Sir," he told Drayton, "if you want me to resign my position, you must call meetings all over the Congressional District and get the people who elected me to pass resolutions requiring me to resign, and then you can have the office without a penny. Otherwise I would suffer myself to go to the Penitentiary and rot before I resign an office that I was elected to." Perhaps the Democrats thought that Smalls would yield to the fury of their public attacks, but they soon discovered that they were dealing with a heart of oak. Like the good pilot that he was, Smalls nailed his colors to the mast and determined to sink with the ship. He refused to resign until he was declared innocent.

After the sentence had been passed by the state court and Smalls sent to jail where he remained for three days, he followed the advice of some of his congressional colleagues and appealed to the Supreme Court of the United States. While the appeal was pending, a deal was made between South Carolina state Attorney

[48] *Constitutional Convention Journal,* 1895, 474.

General Youmans and the United States District Attorney, L. C. Northrop, by which South Carolina promised to drop its charges against Smalls if the United States would drop its charges against South Carolinians accused of violating election laws. This compromise was worked out without Smalls knowledge, and Smalls was in fact infuriated by it. Meanwhile, Smalls received a letter from Governor Simpson granting "a full pardon to the said Robert Smalls." Youmans promptly visited Washington and got the Supreme Court to drop the case because it had already been settled in South Carolina.[49]

By any application of the usual American tradition of legal justice the case against Robert Smalls was entirely political vendetta. The prosecution witness was of questionable character, and his evidence dubious and unconvincing. The readiness with which the Democrats were willing to pardon Smalls and get the case withdrawn from the Supreme Court further weakens the indictment. Even a one-time member of the Investigating Committee, J. C. Sheppard, admitted later that he was willing "that the unhappy circumstances . . . should be blotted from the memory of men." In calmer moments, the Charleston *News and Courier,* ignoring their story of former years, came out in support of Smalls' defense. "It is a simple statement of fact," the paper declared later, "that he was tried at a time and under circumstances that did not tend to assure him a fair trial and that not a few white men in Columbia . . . held the evidence offered to be insufficient to convict him. . . . We believe it *safe* to say that he could not be convicted before a jury of *impartial white men* [sic] anywhere on the same evidence today." In fact, the case against Robert Smalls supports the thesis of a contemporary historian, Frederick Bancroft, that "the average Southerner did not think so much of the corruption which Negro rule entailed as he did of the fact that the blacks ruled; that Sambo [supposedly subservient and childlike blacks] was in power, and that the superior race was humiliated in the last degree."[50]

Beneath the surface of Republican politics in South Carolina

49 *Ibid.,* 475. A copy of the letter detailing the deal is reprinted.
50 *Ibid.,* 478; Charleston *News and Courier,* November 4, 1895; Frederick Bancroft, *The Negro in Politics* (Columbia, 1885), 70.

at this time there was doubtless much that was shocking. Some blacks were not to be outdone by their white counterparts in seizing the opportunity for gain which politics presented. Many traded their control of votes and legal responsibilities for cash or other considerations. Except for the one discredited charge, however, no recorded action of Smalls was ever linked with dishonesty in public matters. On one occasion, Smalls told Woodruff that he would not accept $5000 to vote for the latter, but would do it gladly if he felt Woodruff was qualified. In fact, one might even take it as a tribute to Robert Smalls' honesty that, though he was identified with the "corrupt" Republicans, he emerged from the Reconstruction Era with a reputation which brought statements of contrition from his earlier accusers.[51]

In all these years of political turbulence, Robert Smalls also continued to show great interest in the military affairs of the state. In recognition of these interests, he was promoted in 1873 to Lieutenant Colonel of the Third Regiment, South Carolina State Militia. He was soon elevated to the position of Brigadier-General. Eventually, he was promoted to Major-General of the Second Division, South Carolina Militia, and held this position until relieved by the Democrats in 1877.[52]

As Commander of the Second Division, South Carolina Militia, Smalls was, in August 1876, ordered to call out the militia to put down a riot by the rice workers near the Combahee River. The black workers on the rice plantations had gone on strike because they were being paid in checks which could be redeemed "only in goods bought at exorbitant prices at the stores of the planters."

Smalls went down personally to the strikers. He expressed sympathy for their cause, but warned them against taking the law into their hands as indicated by alleged attempts to obstruct those who went to work. In a later report to Governor Chamberlain, Smalls detailed the inequities of the labor system. Since the checks could be redeemed in goods only, the rice workers could

[51] Cited by Robert N. Woody, ed., "Behind the Scenes in the Reconstruction Legislature of South Carolina: Diary of Josephus Woodruff," *Journal of Southern History* (May 1936), 275.

[52] William H. Quick, *Negro Stars in all Ages of the World* (Richmond, Va., 1898), 402.

not obtain "any of the necessaries of life except through the planters." They were unable to buy medicines or obtain the services of a physician in case of sickness. Moreover, the prices were exorbitant: the workers paid $2.00 per bushel of grits (regular price $1.00); 25¢ per pound for bacon (regular price from 10¢ to 15¢); $1.00 per gallon for molasses (regular price 40¢). The surprising thing about the strike, Smalls continued, was not that it occurred but that "these people have submitted to this imposition so long without murmuring" because "there is no class of laboring people in the United States that would have submitted so long without striking." The evils resulting from the checks, Smalls declared, were, in "some respects . . . worse than the evils of slavery." He was struck by the decorum displayed by the workers. "I found no lawless disposition among the strikers, many of them belonged to the Militia of the State and as such had arms, but not one of them appeared upon the ground with any kind of weapon, except a club or a stick." On the contrary, "I found from forty to sixty white men, mounted and armed with spencer rifles, sixteen shooters and double barrelled shot guns," the presence of whom "did much to alarm and excite the strikers."[53]

Smalls recommended the abolition of the check system as necessary to the restoration of peace among the workers. "The sure road to peace and contentment in the rice fields," he declared, was "good money for honest labor." He also recommended the removal of the trial justice at Gardners Corner who had ordered the forceful arrest of the strike leaders. The trial justice, Smalls explained, was himself a planter who was guilty of issuing the checks to his laborers and could not therefore be impartial in dealing with the workers' complaints. These recommendations, Smalls added, if accepted, would "add to the peace of the rice district, and the prosperity of the laborers." Smalls' recommendations were accepted, and resulted in the amicable settlement of the dispute.[54]

[53] Smalls to Chamberlain, August 24, 1876, Chamberlain Papers, South Carolina Archives, Columbia, South Carolina.
[54] *Ibid.;* also Beaufort *Tribune,* August 23 and September 13, 1876.

Meanwhile, however, Robert Smalls' arena for political activities had moved from South Carolina to Washington, where for much of the time from 1875 and 1886 he would serve as a Congressman from Beaufort.

V

AGAINST THE TIDE:
SMALLS IN CONGRESS, 1875-1886

WHILE MISSISSIPPI had the distinction of sending two blacks to
the United States Senate during the Reconstruction decades,
South Carolina was conspicuous for the number of her black
Representatives. At various times during these years, and largely
as a result of her large and well-organized black population, the
state sent eight blacks to Congress. In 1870 the black population
of the state stood at 415,814 as compared to 289,667 whites; in
1880 it was 604,332 as against 391,105 whites. Blacks outnumbered whites in twenty of the thirty-one counties in the state.[1]

In Beaufort County the blacks outnumbered the whites seven
to one. Ben Tillman contemptuously referred to the county as a
"niggerdom,"[2] and another observer called Beaufort a "black
paradise."[3] Also, though the black population of the county did
not remain monolithically Republican, the black Republicans
in the area, when combined with the Northern whites, were more

[1] Reynolds, *Reconstruction in South Carolina*, 13; Taylor, *Negroes in South
Carolina Reconstruction*, 5.
[2] Charleston *World*, May 12, 1890; Simkins, *Pitchfork Ben Tillman*, 153.
[3] George Campbell, *White and Black: The Outcome of a Visit to the United
States* (London, 1879), 177.

than enough to keep Beaufort a Republican stronghold down to the end of the century.[4]

Throughout the Reconstruction period, Smalls remained the most influential politician in the district. "The men, women and children seem to regard him with a feeling akin to worship," Laura Towne observed. A visitor indicated that, though Smalls was neither very highly educated nor brilliant, he was "a thoroughly representative man among the people" and seemed to have "their unlimited confidence." Even the "redeeming" Democratic administration recognized the enormous influence Smalls exercised over the county and constantly used him as an intermediary between the "Black District" and the government. Smalls' political aspirations profited greatly from this popularity.[5]

Smalls was first elected to Congress in 1874. His opponent, J. P. Epping, campaigned as a "reform" candidate, but Smalls won easily.[6]

When he left Columbia for the nation's capital in 1874, Robert Smalls was thirty-nine, burly, and in the prime of life. Dressed in his new Prince Albert suit and wearing gold-rimmed glasses, he was no longer the dashing young hero. His family had brought added responsibilities. The problems and experiences of South Carolina's turbulent public life had produced a seasoned and sophisticated politician.

He arrived in Washington a few days before the opening of the Forty-fourth Congress on December 6, 1874, and took up residence in a two-bedroom apartment on Second Street. Soon to join him as his private secretary was his first daughter, Elizabeth,

[4] *Ibid.*, 177-178. Campbell in fact argued that "nowhere are the relations between the whites and the blacks better."

[5] Holland, *Towne Letters and Diary*, 289, 292; Campbell, *White and Black*, 361; *National Republican*, July 22, 1878. Two incidents in 1876 illustrate the extent of Smalls' influence over the district. When it was rumored that the black women of Beaufort were going "to have a row in town" on election day in 1876, the white people of the town of Beaufort pleaded with Smalls to intervene, arguing that he alone could best control "your own people here." In the same year, it took the timely intervention of Robert Smalls to bring a strike among the black rice growers to an end. See the Charleston *News and Courier*, August 24, September 5, 8, 9, 1876; Beaufort *Tribune*, August 30 and September 13, 1876; also Chapter IV above.

[6] Columbia *Union Herald*, October 2, 1874.

who had just graduated from Allen's English and Classical School, West Newton, Massachusetts.

As a Congressman, Robert Smalls continued to feel a deep sense of responsibility toward his constituency and race.[7]

As a measure of economy, the House Committee on Appropriations had submitted a report in which it recommended the reduction in the strength of the navy, the sale of certain naval yards, and the construction of one strategically placed naval rendezvous in the South, preferably at Cockspur or Tybee Island in Georgia. Smalls immediately designated Port Royal as the ideal place for the rendezvous, and proceeded to illustrate the advantages of his district over the two suggested spots. He presented letters from the Navy Department and from private citizens in Port Royal familiar with the natural advantages of the harbor. One letter described an incident involving the German ship, the *Berlin*. On one of its several trips to Tybee Island, the ship, loaded with cotton, was forced by bad weather to remain there. Finding the harbor inadequate, the crew looked around for a more suitable anchorage, and were relieved to find the hitherto neglected but very excellent harbor at Port Royal.

With the advantages of Port Royal so clearly illustrated, Smalls sought to enlist congressional support for his effort. To arguments that Tybee had ample fresh water while Port Royal was "entirely of salt water," Smalls answered that "those [The Navy Department] who know more about the two places favor Port Royal which in the opinion of every competent authority offered superior advantages to . . . any other place on the South Atlantic coast." The cost of getting fresh water to Port Royal would be considerably less than the cost of reclaiming either Tybee or Cockspur. Smalls won the argument and Port Royal was chosen as the better location.

He next sought to secure adequate appropriations for improv-

[7] Frederick Turner, David Donald, and very lately Allen Bogue, have in different studies shown the significance of constituency as an important voting determinant for legislators. See Turner, "The Significance of Section in American History," *Wisconsin Magazine of History*, VIII (1925); David Donald, *The Politics of Reconstruction* (Baton Rouge, 1965); Allen Bogue, "Block and Party in the United States Senate, 1861-1863," *Civil War History*, XIII (September 1967), No. 3, 221-241.

ing the port. Since the war, the range lights at the entrance to the harbor had been destroyed. In Smalls' view, $40,000 would be sufficient for such improvement, and he presented a letter from the Secretary of the Navy to support his claim. The Navy Department had in fact estimated that the cost of making the harbor safe for navigation would be about $50,000. Smalls' appropriation motion was thus passed with little debate.[8]

Smalls was next involved in a discussion of the question of security on the Texas frontier and the necessity to remove troops from the South to police the area. A motion had been introduced to authorize the transfer of enlisted men from the infantry to the cavalry, and thus send them to the Texas area. Smalls feared that such a transfer would seriously deplete the force generally responsible for law and order in the Southern states. Frightened by the mounting hostility between the races and convinced that such action as anticipated would be a signal for disorder, Smalls sought to amend the bill so that no troops should be "drawn from the state of South Carolina as long as the militia of that state peacefully assembled are assaulted, disarmed, and taken prisoners, and then massacred in cold blood by lawless bands of men invading that state from the state of Georgia."[9]

In support of his amendment, Smalls presented a letter he had just received from Hamburg, South Carolina, on the recent riots in that city. The riots, according to this source, arose from an attempt by white men to break up a peaceful march of the state militia, composed largely of blacks, on a Fourth of July celebration in the town. After the parade, a black company which had halted to rest was ordered by two white men in a buggy to break ranks and let them pass. Under stubborn pressure, the captain of the company reluctantly acceded to their demands. A few days after, however, the black captain was summoned before the court on a charge of obstructing the public highway. On the day of the trial, bands of white men "armed to the teeth with repeating rifles and revolvers" and led by General M. C. Butler, "one of the most malignant of the unreconstructed rebels," rode into

<hr/>

8 *Congressional Record*, 44th Congress, 1st Session, 3272-75, 4876.
9 *Ibid.*, 4641.

town and took command. Their rank swollen by an influx of white desperadoes from Augusta, Georgia, the "rebels" surrounded the building where the black company was quartered and ordered them to disband or be forced to do so. When the blacks refused, they opened a brisk fire and took twenty of the soldiers to a spot where they organized a "quasi-drumhead court martial." Five were shot in cold blood. In another portion of the town, a black chief of police was dragged from his house and brutally murdered.

These, according to the writer of the letter, were "facts which I vouch for entirely, and are not distorted in any degree. It's a plain unvarnished narration of painful and horrible truths." Whatever polish might have been put on the narrative, there is no doubt that it was a fair representation of what took place. Before the affair took a political turn, the reaction of some moderate whites was that the "men who thus appease their wrath at being detained on the street by the parading negro militiamen" were "guilty of the grossest outrage ever perpetuated in the state." Butler himself admitted that the incident was "a sort of spontaneous combustion" which left many blacks dead.[10] Smalls' amendment was passed, and the President promised to send additional troops to South Carolina if they were needed to keep the peace.

The debate on the issue showed Smalls' mastery of repartee, especially in his exchanges with Samuel Cox, Democrat of Ohio. While the letter was being read, Democrats constantly interrupted to ask for the name of the author. Smalls drew great applause when, in reply to one of these requests, he said: "I will say to the gentleman, if he is desirous that the name shall be given in order to have another negro killed, he will not get it from me." Smalls vouched for the authorship of the letter. This apparently insulting reply drew Cox, the wit of the House, into the argument. Smalls might vouch for the letter, Cox indicated, but who endorsed Smalls? Smalls was equal to the task and replied, "A majority of 13,000." Cox then opened a severe attack on Republican government in South Carolina, quoting exten-

[10] Yorkville *Enquirer*, July 13, 1876; Charleston *News and Courier*, July 18, 1876.

sively from Pike's *The Prostrate State* to prove how corrupt that state's government was. He had read only a few pages, however, when Smalls interrupted to ask: "Have you the book there of the city of New York?" The House rocked with laughter as Cox found himself at a loss to answer. A New York Republican pointed out that nothing in South Carolina could match his own state's record of extravagance and dishonesty under the Democrats.[11]

Some Republican Congressmen came to the defense of Smalls. When Cox referred to Smalls as "somebody of a different color and race," Congressman Hoar of Massachusetts defended and praised the decorum displayed by Smalls and his black colleagues. "They have had to counter the most formidable antagonist [Cox], perhaps the most trained and experienced debater in this House. Yet who can cite an instance of an improper utterance in speech or of an undignified or unbecoming act of a Colored Representative?"[12]

Smalls' exchanges with Representative Charles Hooker of Mississippi were even more bitter. Hooker blamed the Republican party for inciting a race war in South Carolina, and indicated that in the "redeemed states" there was no disturbance. When Hooker asserted emphatically that "there was no friend of the colored man more sincere and more honest than he who was his master when the relations prevailed of master and slave," and that in other states blacks were forming "democratic organizations," Smalls interrupted. "That is not so," he shouted angrily, "the colored people never voted the democratic ticket except under intimidation." Though Hooker offered evidence to substantiate his claims, which were partly correct, and ordered Smalls to "take your seat now, I do not want to be interrupted any further," Smalls shouted back that blacks would never become Democrats "if they were not hunted down by the Ku Klux Klan."[13]

However diffident the freshman Congressman might have been

[11] *Congressional Record*, 44th Congress, 1st Session, 4605-7, 4643.
[12] *Ibid.*, 4641-44.
[13] *Ibid.*, 5383-84; for an examination of the attitude of South Carolina blacks toward the Democratic party, see William W. Ball, *A Boy's Recollection of the Red Shirt Campaign* (Columbia, S.C., 1911); New York *Age*, July 14, 1888.

when he entered the House, the exchanges with Samuel Cox and Hooker must have given him some confidence. Besides, the response of his party to Democratic attacks on him and other blacks was reassuring. Thus emboldened, Smalls introduced several bills to improve the situation in his state and also for the relief of his constituents, black and white. He called for the construction of docks, warehouses, and other buildings for shipping accommodations at Port Royal Harbor and the redemption and sale of the land still held by the Federal Government in his state. He called upon the government to make appropriate compensation for her use of the citadel at Charleston since 1865, and to arrange for the return of this "valuable property" to the people of Charleston or arrange terms for the continued use of the property, should such be necessary. All these measures were passed.[14]

The discussion on the reorganization of the Armed Forces in the interest of economy and efficiency drew Smalls into another heated debate. Among the measures suggested to achieve the desired end were the reduction of the salaries of officers, regulation of promotion to official rank, and the consolidation of certain corps to increase the size of the companies and thus reduce incidental expenses. By far the least objectionable method was retrenchment. Ohio's Representative, Henry Banning, called for the gradual reduction and consolidation of certain staff departments. Perhaps reflecting his racial bias, Banning also demanded the repeal of the Revised Statutes which had provided that the enlisted men of certain regiments should be black. He argued that this would do away "with that odious feature in the law" and make entry into the army solely on merit as in other aspects of the nation's life.

This seemed to the black Representatives to be a mere cloak for the retrenchment of black soldiers and a possible refusal to employ more. Smalls saw through the clever design and sought to amend the bill thus: "That hereafter, in the enlistment of men in the Army or in the merging of enlisted men into other organizations, no distinction whatever shall be made on account

14 *Ibid.*, 442, 2156, 3754, 4161, 1484.

of race, or color." Banning, supported by Representative Samuel J. Fandell of Pennsylvania, objected to Smalls' amendment, and thus lent validity to the fear of the blacks.

Edmund Mackey, a South Carolina white Representative, took up the black cause. "The real object of introducing the bill," he maintained, was "to discontinue entirely the enlistment of colored men." In an earlier speech, he continued, Banning had betrayed his anti-black sentiments when he said that "the experiment with colored troops has proven a disastrous failure," and that "colored men who do enter the army are of such a class they cannot be trusted or made of any benefit to themselves or the country." The sponsors of the bill, he alleged, were "seeking under the guise of a worthy motive to accomplish the unworthy one of practically closing the army against colored men." He made a spirited and moving plea for the right of blacks to enlist in the army if they so desired. To deny them that, he declared, "would be exceedingly unjust in view of the fact that this country has never failed in time of war to call upon these people to fight as soldiers in her defense." He made a quick review of the contribution of black soldiers to American war efforts since the Revolution. "In view of these facts," he concluded, "it is not only extremely unwise but exceedingly ungrateful to close the Army, now that we are at peace with all the world, against these peoples."

Banning charged those who spoke for Smalls' amendment with partisanship, and argued that blacks would enter the Army, just as they won elections to state and national legislatures. Smalls would not agree, and argued that their presence on the floor of Congress was no insurance against discrimination against them in other walks of life. A substitute bill which sought to allow the President to appoint a committee to inquire into the reorganization of the army was defeated. Smalls' amendment was also rejected. Banning's original bill passed by 123 to 82, with Smalls in opposition. The reconciliation between North and South and the consequent abandonment of the blacks were already in the air.[15]

[15] *Ibid.*, 3457-62; 3468-69.

Though he was appointed to the Agricultural Committee, Smalls presented no agricultural bill, but did participate in the discussion of a bill relevant to land use. Benjamin Hill of Georgia had presented a report from the Committee of Ways and Means which sought to extend the time for the redemption of lands held by the government under the direct tax laws to February 1, 1877. Smalls had earlier helped initiate a bill passed December 1875 which had called for the redemption of the lands so held, particularly in South Carolina. The time stipulated in the previous bill had not expired, and the sales of much of the land had already been completed, at least in South Carolina. Smalls therefore felt further legislation on the subject unnecessary, and called for the report to be tabled.

By the time Congress adjourned in August 1876, Smalls had learned much. He had, in the face of great difficulties and the opposition of better educated and seasoned legislators, proven his ability to represent his state and people. Because of his speeches, few newspaper readers in the country did not know the story of the Hamburg "massacres." He had championed the cause of his state, race, and party, but to continue in the fight he would have to win the impending election.

The year 1876 was critical for the Republicans of South Carolina as indeed it was for the rest of the nation. The performance of Governor Chamberlain had endeared him to the South Carolina Republicans because he had lived up to his campaign promises in 1874. During his administration the public debt had been paid off, legislative expenses reduced to save the state $55,000, the character of public officers improved, and confidence in the government restored. Even the opposing Democrats acknowledged the efforts of Chamberlain to advance the cause of good government in the state. At a meeting in Charleston in August 1876, the Democrats expressed appreciation for "the courageous course of Governor Chamberlain in his efforts to stay the ruins which his party has brought upon the state." They gave him "unqualified support for his good work," and there was widespread sentiment, strongly supported by the *News and Courier,* for a coalition to support Chamberlain's re-election. When the Republican state convention presided over by Smalls met, it gladly endorsed Chamberlain's re-election.[16]

Meanwhile, however, some Democrats would not support anything short of the state being delivered completely into the hands of her white citizens. To them, Chamberlain was unacceptable because he had betrayed his race by cooperating with the "black Republicans." With Martin M. Gary as their leader, they called for a "straightout" Democratic campaign, and they won more adherents after two incidents in 1875. The first was the appointment of W. J. Whipper (black) and F. J. Moses, former governor, as circuit judges. Both men had been repeatedly charged with corruption, and despite Chamberlain's refusal to sign the commission of their appointment, the Democrats seized upon the appointment as proof that the Republicans were totally unregenerate. The second incident was the Hamburg riots after which "moderate voices were drowned by the uproar of agitation and vilification." When the Democrats met at a convention in August, they voted to "take it straight," named Wade Hampton, a Confederate hero, as their candidate for governor, and chose a slate composed entirely of white men.[17]

The ensuing fall campaign was notorious for the fradulent practices and violence of both parties. The *News and Courier* was not alone in crying out against "these outrages upon our civilization." "It comes near to home," the paper declared, "when we hear that a venerable citizen, nearly eighty years of age, is fired upon and seriously wounded. Every nerve quivers when we hear of ladies driven from their homes in the dead of night, their path lighted by flames springing from barns and gin-houses, and woods made hideous by shouts of exultant incendiaries." *The Times* commented that Democratic meetings "so impress the blacks with a sense of danger as to render Republican gatherings useless for the purposes they were intended to serve." It deplored interference by Democrats in Republican rallies, maintaining

[16] Charleston *News and Courier*, July 5-9, 12-16, 18, 28, 1876, September 25, 26, 1876, December 21, 1875.

[17] Columbia *Daily Register*, August 18, 1876; Charleston *News and Courier*, September 30, 1876.

that it was difficult to find mention of any Republican meeting which had not been broken up by the Democratic "cavalry." One observer commented that Charleston seemed like a military camp and attributed to the Democrats a plan "to drive Republicans to the well and force them to assume the offensive, when they will then commence a wholesale slaughter of such as refuse to join their political party." On their part, Republicans circulated a paper which called upon the "faithful" in Lawrence County to "burn out any white man, kill his mules . . . kill his hogs and cows—keep him under. Support the constitution or die." The state was so enveloped in fear that only the courageous dared to go out campaigning.[18]

This was the situation when Robert Smalls, in the company of Governor Chamberlain, carried the fight into Edgefield, the very heart of the state's Democratic party. Before the rally, it was obvious that Smalls was detested by the Edgefield people. Within the past few months in Congress he had constantly criticized the district and its leader. The Republicans entered Edgefield, it was later noted, "with a cavalcade of persons, the most obnoxious in the eyes of the people of Edgefield, among them Congressman Smalls who had grossly vilified the white people of Edgefield on the floor of Congress." Others in the group were identified as the progenitors of the then current idea that Edgefield was "the very heart of rebeldom." The visit of such a group was bound to touch off trouble, and it was in fact being rumored that the Republican rally would be "in some way interrupted."[19]

On their arrival, Smalls later testified before the Committee on Recent Elections in South Carolina, the Republican dignitaries found the town gradually filling with crowds of fully-armed white men. Led by Gary and Butler, the men, about six to eight hundred, drove around the town shouting almost continuously "the rebel yell." They proceeded to the square where the Republicans had gathered and demanded "an equal portion of the time of the meeting." When the Republicans refused on the

18 *Ibid.*, September 26 and 30, quoting *The New York Times.*
19 Select Committee on Recent Elections in South Carolina, Charleston, December 30, 1876; House of Representatives, 44th Congress, 2nd Session, Miscellaneous Document 31, part 3, 197-199.

grounds that this was a party meeting called for the ratification of their presidential and vice-presidential candidates, Hayes and Wheeler, General Butler threatened to take it by "fair or foul means." The Democrats would not allow any chairman to be chosen for the occasion, arguing that they wanted "to govern the meeting; it shall be fair and square, and every man shall have thirty minutes to speak."

When Governor Chamberlain was introduced to speak first, the white clubs demanded that General Butler should speak first. They directed a barrage of embarrassing questions at Chamberlain. In his speech, Butler confined himself largely to abusing Chamberlain whom he called "a damn bald-headed renegade and bummer of Sherman's Army, and now so-called governor of South Carolina." He then turned to Robert Smalls "who has used my name in the Halls of Congress as being the leader of the Ku Klux." He dared Smalls "to open his lips on this stand today," as the approving crowd shouted "kill the damn son of bitch! Kill the damn nigger." When Smalls' turn to speak came, the white crowd broke up in an uproar and brought the platform down. "No, that God damn nigger shall not speak here today," they shouted, and threatened to take Smalls' life "if he opens his mouth here today." At about 2 P.M., the meeting broke up. On the way back, Democrats surrounded the train which had brought the Republicans and demanded to know where "that fellow Smalls" was. When "the nigger congressman" was recognized in the car, some demanded to have a lock of his hair; one argued that they should hang him because that "was the only way to keep him from coming back."[20]

Governor Chamberlain later described the incident as "a torrent of abuse of me personally, and an exhibition of force and threats designed to intimidate the colored voters and their leaders." He indicated that on the way home a number of armed men entered the car and with "rude and threatening manners addressed their jeers and insults at General Smalls."[21]

Robert Smalls was not intimidated, however, and made bold

[20] *Ibid.*, 199.
[21] Walter Allen, *Governor Chamberlain's Administration in South Carolina: A Chapter of Reconstruction in the Southern States* (New York, 1888), 374-377.

to attend another Republican meeting at Edgefield. Again, the white mob came, though this time "not so extensively armed." Again, Generals Butler and Gary rode over to the meeting. There was no disturbance, although, when one Republican was speaking, a Democrat said he was "a God damn liar." At another campaign meeting at Allendale, there was "considerable disturbance" when Smalls rose to speak. Throughout the campaign, Smalls received letters threatening his life and property.

On election day, both parties resorted to all kinds of dubious tactics. In Beaufort, the Democrats circulated their ticket, designed as a Republican list, to confuse the large Republican electorate. Only the timely intervention of Smalls revealed this fraud. He quickly moved to the different precincts in his constituency circulating the proper Republican ticket.

According to one contemporary, the election was "one of the greatest farces ever seen." "Terror and fraud were used on both sides," a later historian commented, "and the vote so affected by these tactics that no one will ever know what the outcome would have been in a fair and honest election." The result was a stalemate in which the executive branch of the state government ground to a halt. The Democrats, however, with the cooperation of the Federal Government, accomplished their purpose, and South Carolina joined the ranks of the "redeemed states" of the South.[22]

When Wade Hampton became governor in 1876, the ambitious experiment launched in the Sea Islands in 1862 came to an end. For, although Hampton had declared emphatically that his employment policy "depended on a man's competency and his conduct, if he was capable and did his duties faithfully," there was a limit to which he could go without offending the prevalent racial attitudes. No doubt, Hampton did appoint blacks as trial justices and jury commissioners, including a black businessman from Beaufort, R. H. Gleaves, and the old abolitionist, Martin R. Delany. So apparently liberal was Hampton in making black

[22] A South Carolinian, "The Political Condition of South Carolina," *Atlantic Monthly*, XXXIX (February, 1877), 187; Tindall, *South Carolina Negroes*, 14; Reynolds, *Reconstruction in South Carolina;* Henry T. Thompson, *Ousting the Carpetbagger from South Carolina* (Columbia, S.C., 1926).

appointments that former Governor Robert Scott told a news-paperman in Ohio a year after he took office that "Hampton . . . has already appointed more colored men to office than were appointed during the first two years that I was governor." Actually, however, these black appointments can best be seen as an attempt to weaken the widespread discontent of black people. Significantly, the *News and Courier* observed that an "endeavor is being made to avoid putting colored persons in positions where they would, or could be peculiarly offensive."[23]

Moreover, given the dominant spirit of the times, with both Northern and Southern white opinion accepting as axiomatic the innate inferiority of black peoples, Hampton's liberal attitude was countered by serious opposition at the grass roots. Resolutions were passed by various Democratic clubs barring black people from participation in Democratic meetings. An Edgefield Democratic convention, after hearing a "straightout Edgefield speech" by Martin Gary, resolved that "we regard the issue between the white and the colored people of this state . . . as an antagonism of race not a difference of political parties. White supremacy is essential to our continued existence as a people." To admit blacks into the Democratic party, the Spartan-burg *Spartan* declared, would "not only destroy the controlling influence of the white man, and endanger his institutions and civilizations, but will put the up-country of South Carolina under the control of the low country, where the great negro vote lies." Hampton might have been "in a class by himself," as the blacks said in the state, but the "just and liberal course of the Governor," was soon eclipsed by the open avowal for white supremacy represented by the Gary faction. A Northern correspondent understood the situation very well when he observed that:

> When it comes to an election or to any exercise of the right of suffrage, the Democratic party steps in and takes charge of things. The negro is bulldozed and intimidated, and his vote is thrown out of the ballot box after he has contrived to get it in. This done, and the

23 See Hampton M. Jarrel, *Wade Hampton and the Negro: The Road Not Taken* (Columbia, S.C., 1949); Columbia *Daily Register,* November 1, 1878; Charleston *News and Courier,* June 20 and April 14, 1877; Yorkville *Enquirer,* September 26, 1878.

object attained, the Butlers and the Garys retire, and all is once more moderation and conciliation.[24]

In fact, after 1876, the black man was merely a political cipher in South Carolina.

Robert Smalls was not, however, swept out by the counter-revolution. Even in these years of reversals in political fortunes, the black majority of Beaufort County remained true to Smalls and delivered whatever votes they still had to him. He plunged into the bitter state campaign in 1876. Opposition, especially when it was strong, seemed to stiffen his determination to win and to spur him to prodigious energy. His record in the previous Congress, especially as it reflected his interest in the welfare of his people, also contributed to Smalls' success in the campaign. "He is not a man of culture and oratorial ability like Lynch [black Congressman from Mississippi]," one paper that publicly endorsed Smalls declared, "but he is a very fair representative of his race." Smalls' constituents were grateful for his efforts in Washington and admired his courage in South Carolina. His campaign was well organized, and the over-all "redeemer" victory did not prevent his re-election. His defeated opponent contested the election on the grounds that he was fradulently beaten, but after a spirited discussion, Smalls was confirmed. The Democratic House was apparently in no mood to exasperate the already critical situation in South Carolina by denying Smalls the seat.[25]

Up to 1876, black Republican Robert Brown Elliot had towered above all the other members of the South Carolina congressional delegation. Described by hostile critics as "the exponent of the lowest and most oppressive form of South Carolina Radicalism," and by friendly commentators as a "splendid intellect, improved by the best training," Elliot was widely recognized as

[24] Thomas Miller to Theodore D. Jarvey, December 19, 1927, Woodson Papers; Charleston *News and Courier,* June 4, 20 and July 17, 1878, quoting the *Spartan;* Campbell, *White and Black,* 330; Edward Hogan, "South Carolina To-Day," *International Review,* VIII (February 1880), 109; also Tindall, *South Carolina Negroes,* 22-40.
[25] Charleston *News and Courier,* December 13, 1876; Reynolds, *Reconstruction in South Carolina,* 362, 366; *World Almanac,* 1877; Smith, *Negro in Congress,* 69, 98; Miscellaneous Newspaper Clippings, Moorland Foundation, Howard University.

the most adroit as well as the ablest black representative from
South Carolina. By 1876, however, Elliot's meteoric career was
drawing to a rapid close, and he was succeeded in party influence
by Smalls.[26]

The short session of 1876-77 was practically consumed in discussion of the election of 1876. The disputed count in South
Carolina, together with the struggle over the governorship, was
also a subject for heated debate. Smalls seized the opportunity to
comment on the "unfortunate division existing among the people
of my state as to who is the lawfully elected governor of the
state and who were the lawfully elected presidential electors."[27]

Though essentially a campaign document, this prepared speech,
titled "An Honest Ballot Is the Safeguard of the Republic,"
throws much light on Smalls' view of the white race, black people,
the political tension in the state, and Republican rule in South
Carolina. "The white race of South Carolina," Smalls declared,
possessed "intelligence and courage." The existence of slavery
had cemented their personal interests and compelled them to act
in concert in political matters. Because of his relationship with
the slave, the master became domineering in spirit and disposed
"to ignore and trample the rights of those they could not control." They became "cruel, refusing education to, and ignoring
the sanctity of the family relations of their slaves." The doctrine
of a slave having rights was anathema to them. "They never
learned to recognize such a principle and would tolerate no free
expression of opinion" on the matter.

The blacks, on the other hand, Smalls continued, under normal
circumstances, were "gentle, patient, and affectionate; possessed
of no cruel impulses . . . a harmless race, generous to a fault,"
and their confidence was easily won. Smalls attributed these

26 Charleston *News and Courier*, September 19, 1876; Reynolds, *Recon-*
struction in South Carolina, 259, 366; *Atlantic Monthly* (April 1901); Thompson, *Ousting the Carpetbagger*, 107. Carter Woodson thought Elliot was the
most brilliant of the Negro Representatives in Congress. Frederick Douglass
said of him, "I have known but one other Negro to be compared with Elliot
and that was S. R. Ward." Cited in Smith, *Negro in Congress*, 60-61.

27 "An Honest Ballot Is the Safeguard of the Republic," Speech of Hon.
Robert Smalls in the House of Representatives, February 24, 1877, *Congres-*
sional Record, 44th Congress, 2nd Session, Appendix, 123-136.

qualities to long years of suffering as slaves and "bitter lessons of experience." The white people had degraded the slave's manhood and "reduced him to a condition of ignorance through centuries of enforced subjection." After the Civil War black political and human rights were recognized by the constitution of the country. For once the black man was emancipated from the condition of complete dependence upon his master, and was set for playing his rightful role in the affairs of the nation.

Smalls admitted that two such political elements as widely different in character as the blacks and the former slaveholders of the South could not co-exist without much antagonism. The granting of suffrage to blacks had originated a new and controlling element in the Southern states. Afraid of losing their control, the Southern whites were determined to restore the status quo ante bellum, and could do this only by depriving the black man of his newly won rights. "The late slave holding class," Smalls correctly declared, "would not submit peacefully to a government they could not control, believing they are a superior race." Since they did not recognize the rights of the colored man, Smalls added, they felt justified in resorting to any means in their power to accomplish their end. Thus, human life was taken with impunity; citizens were driven from their homes; fraud was perpetrated.

Though he recognized the tension as inevitable, Smalls was shocked at the lack of decorum displayed by the whites in accomplishing their purpose. "It never entered the minds of the most apprehensive," he argued "that the white race would resort to such inhuman brutality to recover power." He continued:

> When it was considered their cruelty was against a harmless race, it affords no defense, and their course becomes the blacker in comparison with their boasted chivalry, their claim of superior gentleness, and of those virtues which adorn the human race.[28]

He called the attention of the "civilized world" to what crimes were being perpetrated against the blacks in the South. He would have the American people compare the "manner by which

28 *Ibid.*

a rebellious people were treated by a generous government, and
in turn the treatment of the Negro race by the pardoned class."
He praised black people for remaining "peaceful under such trying circumstances." "The blood of the innocent freedmen, shed
by Southern Democrats would," he argued, "in future prove one
of the dark spots upon the fair name of the American Republic."

Smalls discounted the argument of James S. Pike in *The Prostrate State* and of Southern whites to justify the agitation for
"redeeming" the Southern states. Corruption and extravagance,
he admitted, certainly existed in some of the states. But in South
Carolina the administration of Governor Chamberlain, which
the Democrats were pledged to drive from the seat of power,
"had been one of marked reform, of a character to command
the admiration of every citizen." Expenditures and salaries had
been reduced; the abuse of the pardoning power had been cor-
rected; men of better character had been appointed to office; the
tax laws had been amended to secure unanimity of assessment
and taxation; the contingent fund of the executive had been
reduced by $101,200, the legislative expenses by $350,810, the
expenses of public printing by $512,418, and taxes from thirteen
and one-half mills to eleven mills. He quoted the Charleston
News and Courier, "the voice of the majority of the democrats in
the state," to substantiate his claims. After careful scrutiny, the
Courier had presented "hard figures and unmistakable facts" to
show that the record as it stood was one of which Governor
Chamberlain had "cause to be proud," and justified the support
given him and was "a complete answer" to those who thought
that no act of Governor Chamberlain deserved "public commen-
dation." The reforms accomplished by Governor Chamberlain,
Smalls reminded the House, had been endorsed by his party
which in fact had entered the 1876 campaign "pledged to reform
and good movement." Given this record, Smalls argued, the
charge of corruption and extravagance was just a cloak for the
real reason—that South Carolina wanted a "whiteman's government." For despite all the Democratic charges of corruption,
"whenever a man rose superior to the corruption in his party,
be he a native republican or otherwise, he became an object of
abuse and villification. The more he endeavored to accomplish

for good government the worse the abuse he would receive, and often the crime of doing good for himself and his people merited the punishment of death."

To Smalls, the election of 1876 was an illustration of designs of the Democrats to negate the black man's political power. He charged upon that party in South Carolina murder, violence, and intimidation, especially in Barnwell, Abbeville, Edgefield, and Laurens counties, the centers of serious racial clashes during the previous campaign; he accused the Democrats of turning the day of election into a carnival of bloodshed and violence, violating the purity of the ballot box by unblushing fraud, sanctioned by the entire party, from candidate down to voter; and, above all, of striking a second blow at the "perpetuity of American institutions by inaugurating in the centennial year the practice of securing by fraud, and murder what could not be obtained by honorable means." Indicating confidence in the judgment of the American people, "the great tribunal that has always been ready to lend a helping hand to the oppressed," Smalls expressed a hope that the future would do much to "obliterate the stain upon the fair name of South Carolina and the disgrace to American civilization." Once the constitutional rights of the blacks were respected, they would, "actuated by the purpose to prove worthy of American citizenship, pursue their way peacefully, resolved to be patriotic citizens of a great country." "The ballot in the hands of the black man," Smalls reminded a House that appeared to be forgetting the words of the martyred Lincoln, "may serve in some trying hour to come to preserve the jewel of liberty to the diadem of the Republic."[29]

As one would expect of a campaign document, the speech was partisan. Smalls' claim that twenty-five thousand Georgians crossed into South Carolina and voted was much exaggerated. Substantially, however, it would appear that Smalls' more important points were true. In later years, when memories of Reconstruction had faded and a new compromise between North and South had made pretense over the Negro question unnecessary, a prominent South Carolina Democrat who had been directly involved

[29] *Ibid.*, 124-125.

in the whole struggle testified openly to the extremely undemocratic means employed by the Democrats to "redeem" the state. "We stuffed the ballot boxes," Ben Tillman told the national Senate in 1902. "We shot Negroes. We are not ashamed of it."[30]

Smalls' speech was constantly interrupted with applause from the Republican side of the House. But even as he finished detailing the inhuman treatment of his people in the 1876 campaign, South Carolina was preparing for another election that would rival the previous one in revealing the determination of white South Carolinians in the Democratic party to destroy pockets of black political power in the state.

In 1878, politics was still an arena of deadly combat for blacks in "redeemed" South Carolina. The continued electoral successes of Robert Smalls were not only an offense to the Democrats, but also a commentary on the "impurity" of the redemption. Defeated in 1876, the Democrats in Smalls' district had been organizing for a political showdown in 1878. Fraud, intimidation, and even violence which had been used in 1876 had proved more damaging then effective, and they had to be supplemented by other methods. Speaking in Edgefield in August 1878, Martin Gary repeated his "humble judgment" that Democratic leaders were making a mistake in "considering the differences between Negro and white a difference of politics, instead of a difference in point of fact of race." He called for white unity against the "Black District." Supporters of Governor Hampton would not go that far, but they found nothing wrong in employing all kinds of dubious legalistic means to make Smalls' district "secure." Numerous voting precincts in large Republican counties were abolished. This in effect meant disfranchisement of many black Republican voters who then had to walk several miles to vote and in some places to cross rivers. Many of course did not bother to do so. Republican districts were gerrymandered to create safe Democratic enclaves.[31]

"Political times are simply frightful," Laura Towne wrote from the Sea Islands as election day approached. "Men are shot

---

[30] Smith, *Negro in Congress*, 69; Patrick, *Reconstruction of the Nation*, 300.
[31] Charleston *News and Courier*, August 8, 15, 1878; *Appleton's Annual Cyclopaedia*, III (1878).

at, hounded down, trapped and held till certain meetings are over, and intimidated in every possible way." A white editor in Smalls' district called upon Democrats to rally round to defeat Smalls and argued that *"any* measure that will accomplish the end will be justifiable, *however wicked* [sic] they might be in other communities."[32]

Though Smalls was enthusiastically received by his audiences, it was soon evident that he was facing a herculean task. For many in the black district the last two years had been a nightmare, while the future could be imagined only as a projection of the hopeless present. Many blacks would rather stay home than brave the vengeance of the Democratic cavalry. Some black leaders who greeted Smalls' successes with enthusiasm soon proved to be self-seeking, ready to displace Smalls as a political leader and cash in on the situation. Moreover, sober reflection on Smalls' part should have convinced him of the ultimate political cost of his recent indictment and trial. A community fed on frightful rumors of danger to the personal safety of its people was hardly suitable for the kind of political campaign Smalls needed.

Smalls was badly hampered in his campaigns by the interference of Democrats. At Blackville he addressed an audience of about three hundred black supporters and similar number of white Democrats. He told Laura Towne of an incident at Gillisonville, in the new county of Hampton carved out of Beaufort, where he made a campaign appearance. When he arrived in the city at ten in the morning, he found about forty supporters gathered at the meeting place and groups coming up the street to attend the meeting. Suddenly, a large number of whites rode into town, giving the "real rebel yell" and "whooping like Indians." They took positions on the outskirts of the crowd, and, every few minutes, a squad of three or four would set down the street and "lick off the hats of .the colored men" and slap the faces of the women coming to the meeting. Smalls with some difficulties restrained his supporters from counterattacking. The leader of the white group then insisted that there should be a joint session and each party given half of the meeting. Smalls

32 Holland, *Towne Letters and Diary,* 288-289.

instead withdrew with some of his supporters into a nearby store. The whites surrounded them and fired several shots into the building and threatened to set it afire. The alarm spread in all directions, and blacks from the countryside, armed with guns, axes, and hoes, began to converge on the town. The whites galloped away and a major riot was narrowly averted.[33]

Election day was another panorama of fraud, intimidation, and violence. One visitor reported that he found the first station he came to full of people "dressed in the famous red shirts." He noticed a "good deal of talking and shouting and galloping about on horseback and some few symptoms of whisky." Governor Wade Hampton later regretted "the wrongfulness and absolute impolicy" of the methods used by his party in that election. Robert Smalls, the chief target, of course lost his congressional seat to George Tillman. Significantly, however, 909 of the 910 black voters in St. Helena Island voted for Smalls, thus showing that not black disenchantment, but white fraudulence cost Smalls the election. In fact, the black people were "greatly grieved about it," and were "not reconciled to the result." Smalls himself was philosophic, arguing that "the outrageous bulldozing and cheating in this last election is the best thing that could have happened for the Republican party, for it has been so barefaced and open that it cannot be denied, and so much depends upon having Republicans in Congress now . . . that it will not be negligently passed over, as it has been before."[34]

Undiscouraged by his defeat and convinced that it was far from the expression of the popular will, Smalls spent the next two years preparing for another contest. Increasing black disenchantment with the Republican party with which Smalls was inextricably identified made this difficult. Fear of re-enslavement, which had wedded the blacks to the Republicans, was receding through more than a decade of freedom.[35] Discouraged by successive

[33] Holland, *Towne Letters and Diary,* 289-291.

[34] *Ibid.,* 293, 358; Campbell, *White and Black,* 312, 313, 316, 258; Yorkville *Enquirer,* January 23, 1879.

[35] For an account of the use made of this fear by both parties in their appeals to the black voters, see "A South Carolinian," *Atlantic Monthly* (February 1877), 193; Columbia *Daily Register,* November 15, 1884; Charleston *News and Courier,* November 22, 1884.

electoral defeats since 1876, burdened with an exaggerated record of corruption and extravagance, and identified as a vehicle for the imposition of "foreign" influences on South Carolina, Republicanism was increasingly becoming an unattractive political umbrella for many blacks. With the party deserted by many whites because of its close identification with the blacks, the sun of Republican political fortunes in South Carolina was setting.

For Smalls, however, the wedlock with Republicanism would not end in divorce. He attended the party's state convention at Columbia on September 3, 1880, but the party was in such disarray that it could not nominate a state ticket for the impending gubernatorial race. In a telling speech, former congressman R. B. Elliot indicated the folly of attempting to run in that election. "Let us not encourage hopes in the breasts of our constituents that are to be blasted," he appealed to the delegates. Given the strength and power at the disposal of the Democrats, he argued, it would be better for them "to fight the enemy by detail than to rush into a pitched battle under the disadvantageous circumstances with certain defeat before them." He also advised against the running of congressional candidates.[36]

Smalls would not yield to such a cowardly course. The party might decide not to run a state ticket, but he was determined to make a congressional race. When it was clear Smalls would not yield, the chairman of the Beaufort Republican party declared that even if he was willing to support a congressional ticket, he would not support the candidacy of Robert Smalls because Smalls "was totally unfit for the position." He even promised to work against Smalls' election should his candidacy be sustained by the party. The announcement created a flutter of excitement, but Smalls remained unmoved.

Undismayed, Smalls opened a vigorous campaign. Once more, the Democrats were determined to stop him. The Beaufort County Democratic chairman, J. W. Barnwell, appealed to the people to repudiate Smalls. He reminded them of the "inestim-

[36] Charleston *News and Courier,* September 4 and 6, 1880. James W. Patton discusses the factors in the decline of the Republican party in the state in "The Republican Party in South Carolina, 1876-1895," *Essays in Southern History,* Fletcher M. Green, ed. (Chapel Hill, N.C., 1949).

able blessings" that had accrued to them by their breaking with the Republican party. The main theme of his campaign was a diatribe against Republicanism with Mr. Republican of the area, Robert Smalls, as the chief target. Often, there were the usual clashes when Democrats rode to break up Republican meetings.

Against these odds, Smalls carried on his campaign. He constantly charged Democrats with broken pledges, prostitution of the electoral system, and with inciting a war between the races. Prominent Republicans refused to speak at any meeting held to advocate the election of Smalls, and Whipper, the one prominent man who campaigned actively for Smalls, brought with him a reputation for dishonesty. The *News and Courier* declared Smalls to be "of the same mind" with Whipper and lavishly praised those who deserted Smalls. The paper saw such desertions as a "sign of awakening sense" and of their being "ashamed of Smalls."[37]

As expected, the official returns from the elections showed Tillman over Smalls by about 8000 votes. Smalls, convinced that this was merely a repeat performance of 1878, decided to contest the election.

The contested election, Smalls vs. Tillman, evoked one of the most heated debates in the Forty-seventh Congress. Republican James Briggs of New Hampshire opened by illustrating how national and state election laws had been negated to secure Tillman's victory. He cited instances from the evidence collected by a special House Committee for the election to show how fraud, intimidation, double voting, prevention of Republicans from voting because "they were minors," and other questionable methods were employed, especially in Hampton, Barnwell, Colleton and Edgefield counties, where black voters outnumbered white. He urged the House to disregard the votes from these counties—a proposition which would have given Smalls 14,393 votes to Tillman's 12,904. Another Republican described the conduct in South Carolina as "villainy."[38]

Democrats attacked Republican deductions from the evidence

[37] *Ibid.,* October 4, 1880.
[38] Smalls v. Tillman, *Congressional Record,* 47th Congress, Appendix, 634-643.

and charged Briggs with playing on the sentiments of the House
to incite sympathy for Smalls because the latter was black. "Admit
that a man is not to be considered as false even though he lives
in South Carolina and has the misfortune to have a white instead
of black skin, and happens to be a Democrat instead of a Republican," Representative Gibson Atherton of Ohio argued in
support of Tillman. He maintained that it was natural that
"excitement should ensue, that some acts of violence should take
place, and arming in self-defense was both inevitable and completely justifiable." Another Democrat argued that he would
rather accept the testimony of the Tillmanites because "allow-
ance should be made for the disparity between the colored and
white race in intelligence and all the elements which constitute
power and capacity to manage, control, and govern." What happened in South Carolina was justifiable in his view because
"great power is always used for the purposes of advantage and
control, in political as well as in other matters, against the weaker
class." Moreover, he would not have the white people of this
country in any state, "whatever the disparity of their numbers
may be," ever submit "to the domination of the inferior race."
The events in South Carolina were in fact in accordance with the
"great universal law of nature—the inevitable law of the survival of the fittest."

As the debate drew on, George Tillman was allowed to speak
for himself. He alleged that his interest was about to be sacrificed on the altar of "infernal sectionalism and partyism," because he knew the Republican-controlled House would seat
Smalls. He warned the party, however, that it would fail in its
effort "either to make white men out of negroes or negroes out
of white men." By turning him ("the representative that the
worth and virtue of the state had chosen") down, the Republicans
would be perpetrating "a great wrong upon the people of this
country."[39]

Two motions, one seeking to seat Tillman, the other Smalls
were then introduced. The Tillman motion lost by a very close
vote, and it took the vote of the speaker for the Smalls motion

39 Ibid., 1st Session, 1882, 6213-6217; 6219-6222.

to pass. In the latter case, the Democrats filibustered and refused to vote.[40]

Undoubtedly, party loyalty played a prominent part in this
triumph of Smalls. On the bases of the evidence, however, Smalls
had a strong case, though some of Smalls' supporters used errone-
ous arguments like the one that all blacks always voted Republican. The Tillmanites, however, did not attempt to deny the
alleged election irregularities but limited their defense to appeals
calculated to exploit inherent racism and the new harmony between the North and the South.

The session was almost ended when Smalls was seated. In the
short remaining time, he successfully introduced a bill for the
erection of a custom house, a post office, and other government
buildings in Beaufort. He also spoke in support of a rejected
Senate bill to appropriate $30,000 for the establishment and
completion of a coaling-dock and naval storehouse at Port Royal.
This, he argued, would ease congestion at the Port which was
fast becoming a great outlet for the immense grain products of
the West on their way to Europe.

The increasing frustration over their failure to carry Smalls'
district had, before the 1878 election, led the Democrats to carve
out Hampton County from Beaufort District. This left what
remained of Beaufort District completely black and Republican,
but hemmed in on all sides by hostile Democratic districts. In
the new Beaufort District, therefore, Republican nomination
was equivalent to election, if any considerable number of blacks
cared to vote. The main contest in the district therefore centered
on the nomination rather than the election.

At a Republican convention which met to nominate candidates
for the 1882 election, a triangular fight developed between a
white, E. M. Mackey, and two blacks, Samuel Lee and Robert
Smalls. At the opening of the convention the relative delegate
strength of the contestants was Mackey fifteen, Lee fourteen, and
Smalls ten. In placing Mackey's name in nomination, a black
delegate impressed upon the convention that the candidate had
always been an uncompromising foe of Bourbon rule in South

[40] *Ibid.*, 6225-26; 6233-34.

Carolina, and that, while other whites were deserting the party and the cause, Mackey remained steadfast and loyal. The blacks could show him no better gratitude than to nominate him for the election. Sammy Green, who nominated Smalls, urged the convention to seize the opportunity then offered to the black people "to run one district at least in their exclusive interest." It was contrary to the principles of black Republicanism, he declared, that, "when by the grace of the Democracy, one district had been given to the colored people, a candidate not representing the race on color principles in the district should invade it for the purpose of capturing all that was left of the Republican party in the state." The speech was vociferously cheered by the Lee delegation, because, apart from being obviously aimed at Mackey, it would throw the strength of Smalls' supporters behind Lee. For Smalls would not go that far in drawing the color line and was suspected of having a deal with Mackey.

When the balloting began, Mackey received his fifteen votes, Lee fourteen, Smalls ten. On the thirty-fifth ballot, there was no change. Though the least favored, Smalls remained confident that, in the event of a deadlock which appeared inevitable, and in view of charges and countercharges which were getting the front runners into more and more inextricable muddles, the black delegates would be unable to resist his appeal. Moreover, there was an understanding between Smalls and Mackey that in case of a deadlock the delegates of one would support the candidate most likely to win the election against Lee. Lee had in fact charged Smalls with a conspiracy to pack the convention against him.

The convention, which was scheduled to last a few days, stretched into a full week, and there was still no choice of a candidate. On the two hundred and forty-seventh ballot, Smalls decided to break the deadlock by supporting Mackey and thus assured the latter's nomination as a white candidate for the "Black District."[41]

Smalls' motive for supporting Mackey against his fellow black, Lee, throws much light on the political philosophy of Robert

41 Charleston *News and Courier,* September 23-28, 1882.

Smalls. Apart from the charge of corrupt bargain which he could not substantiate, Lee also argued that Smalls' delegates had been bribed to support Mackey. The convention, he said, had been "captured by money and other influences." On the floor of the convention, when it was clear they were losing, the Lee delegation introduced a resolution seeking to nullify the nomination of any candidate secured by "bribery and other corrupt means" and to rule such a candidate out as "unworthy the suffrage of a free people." In support of the resolution, Lee presented an alleged promisory note in which Mackey supposedly agreed to pay one delegate two hundred and fifty dollars for his vote. On his own, Mackey constantly charged Lee and his delegates with corruption and using the pulpits of the African Methodist Church to make racial appeals to the delegates.[42]

There is no evidence that Smalls supported Mackey for any reason but the sake of party unity. Nobody charged him with bribery, and it can be safely assumed that the Lee delegates would have missed no evidence to implicate Smalls. In fact, when Lee produced the alleged note and all the Mackey delegates sprang to their feet and rushed over to Lee's side of the hall to snatch the note, it took the timely intervention of Smalls to avert a riot. "By the Eternal God," Smalls shouted, "if any man gets that note, he'll have to march over my dead body."

Smalls was simply doing his best to prevent the disintegration of the "party of Lincoln" in its only enclave in South Carolina. By 1882, the local party had been torn not only by internal dissension but also by racial antagonism. Even as the convention was sitting, the feeling was growing that unless something was done a bloody confrontation with racial overtones might develop between the supporters of the rival candidates. Lee had made an appeal to Smalls' racial feelings, had offered to share his salary with Smalls, and had promised Smalls a job if Smalls would support him, but Smalls had turned the offer down. Mackey, who was white but married to a black woman, seemed to Smalls to be more likely to restore racial harmony within the party than Lee, who openly advocated a racial showdown.

[42] *Ibid.*, September 30, 1882.

The results of the election proved Smalls correct. Urged by his supporters to appeal to the "ballot box against Mackey's bribery and corruption," Lee entered the election as an independent candidate. The Democrats saw no chance of success and entered no candidate. Lee, however, went down in defeat and thus proved that even the voters of the "Black District" demanded more than just being black from their candidates.[43]

Though Smalls' failure in his bid for nomination and election in 1882 indicated that he was no longer all-powerful, the victory of Mackey showed that Smalls still held the balance of power in the district. When Mackey died on January 28, 1884, Smalls was elected without opposition to take his place.[44]

In this Congress, Smalls spearheaded a fight to secure a refund of the direct taxes levied on South Carolina during the Civil War. The direct tax laws had provided that where the amount realized from the confiscated and sold property of any state exceeded the quota imposed on the state, such a state could claim one-fourth of such excesses. Under the law, the quota imposed on South Carolina was $363,570, but the proceeds from sales in the state had amounted to $377,061. The governor of the state had asked for a refund, and the Treasury Department, after proper investigation, recommended that Congress make an appropriation of about $60,000 for this purpose.[45]

Smalls seized the opportunity of a debate over the desirability of such returns to argue that the whole amount collected from the state should in fact be refunded. He justified his position by pointing out the free services the state, especially in the Port Royal area, had rendered to the invading Federal forces during the war. When the army landed, Smalls argued, and before the direct taxes were levied, "every house in the whole town of Beaufort that was suitable was used for hospital purposes." If the owners of such houses should claim rent for their property, the amount would more than settle South Carolina's quota of the taxes. Moreover, the government was still keeping part of

43 *Ibid.*, November 9, 1882.

44 *Ibid.*, September 28, 1882; *Tribune Almanac*, 1885.

45 *Congressional Record*, 48th Congress, 1st Session, House Executive Document No. 40, 5201-3.

the landed property for military and naval purposes without paying taxes on it. It was therefore proper that the amount asked for by the governor should be paid back, and more if possible. Smalls' plea fell on deaf ears, however, and even the Treasury recommendation was rejected on the grounds that South Carolina's insurrectionary sister states had paid back less than half of the four-million-dollar taxes imposed on them during the war.

In the next session of Congress, the important question of segregation on public transportation came up. James O'Hara, a black Representative from North Carolina, introduced a bill providing for equal accommodation for the races on public transportation. Representative Charles Crisp of Georgia offered an amendment to allow any railroad company to provide separate but equal accommodation for white and black persons. Crisp argued that "though all men are equal before the law" and have "the right to demand at the hands of a common carrier as good accommodations and as good services as any other man receives for the same compensation," railroads should not be forced to "carry white people and colored people in the same cars." A law which forced the carriers to do so would go even further than the Civil Rights Act of 1875 or "social equality law" which had been declared unconstitutional by the Supreme Court in 1883 and would "agitate anew" the whole race question.[46]

Robert Smalls disagreed. Black people, he argued, had no objection to riding in a separate car when the car was of the same character as that provided for whites. In the state of Georgia, however, it was more than that. There, blacks were confined to riding in second-class cars even when they bought a first-class ticket. Black passengers with first-class tickets in transit through Georgia were similarly forced to ride in a Jim Crow car which was placed next to the locomotive. Besides, on the roads one always found "a crowd" coming into the cars at stations and "not very politely" ordering the blacks to get out. Smalls indicated that such a thing did not happen in his native state, where there was "a statute providing for proper accommodations for the colored people, and no distinction made among persons travel-

46 *Ibid.*, 2nd Session, 316.

ling through." He appealed especially to "the good sense of those Democrats who are now crying out they are going to be the best friends of the colored men." He called upon "the right thinking Democrats of the House" to join the Republicans in voting down the amendment; he spoke`flatteringly of Cleveland, "that great and good man, who is going to be our next President [and] will do all that is best for the welfare of the colored people." It was improper, he concluded, to say that black people "shall have nothing but a Jim Crow car in Georgia."

James O'Hara pleaded for harmony and the removal of the race question from the debates. "I for one," he declared, "hold that we are all Americans; that no matter whether a man is white or black he is an American citizen and that the aegis of this great Republic should be held over him regardless of his color." The race question, however, was too central to Democratic policies in the South and fitted too well into the intellectual currents of the time to be so lightly dismissed. The theory of social Darwinism was in vogue, the white man's burden was justifying the carving of empires in Asia and Africa, and many Anglo-Saxon Americans could not afford to be too kind to the black "colonies" in their midst. Moreover, the race question was central to the increasing harmony between North and South. Thus, the wishes of Crisp who spoke for the New South rather than those of James O'Hara the Negro had to be respected. Clifton Breckenridge of Arkansas introduced a substitute amendment to allow the railroads "the right to classify passengers as they may deem best for the public comfort and safety, or to relate to transportation between points wholly within the limits of one state." The substitute amendment passed 137 to 131 with 55 not voting.[47]

In the autumn of 1884, Robert Smalls won his last electoral victory in a campaign which clearly showed what an expert in the political game he had become. Opposed by a Confederate veteran, William Elliot, Smalls tried to be conciliatory whenever the whites were present in numbers but in other places he harangued the blacks. On October 18, a Republican rally met at Beaufort to counteract the effects of a Democratic rally earlier in

[47] *Ibid.,* 317-321.

the day. Smalls' old adversary, the Charleston *News and Courier,* described his speech on that occasion as "a piteous appeal to his friends not to desert him, who had fought on the Federal side for the Democratic candidate who had fought on the Confederate side." He fumed and sweated, the paper continued, and besought "in anxious expression and humiliating utterances" for their continued support. He paraded and stalked up and down the stage "as if in frantic desperation that in this very citadel the Democrats had demoralized his garrison and had produced such an impression as was hard to obliterate, and that by desertion of his troops and the valor of the storming party the honors of the Seventh District were likely to be bestowed upon an able representative of their own number." Some days earlier before a predominantly black audience, Smalls had harangued Elliot and accused him of a crime he was not able to substantiate. This time he publicly apologized to Elliot whom, he admitted, he had charged falsely. "The change in his mode and manner of speech," the *Courier* commented, "was most noticeable, and he exhausted the most strenuous efforts to undermine the [Democratic] day's work." The paper was apparently pleased with Smalls' manliness in publicly retracting the charges he had earlier made against Elliot. Other speakers on the occasion were not that concilia-tory. W. J. Whipper's speech was "in the usual strain of bitter denunciation and invective against the Democratic party gener-ally, and towards the several state officers particularly." The state judiciary was also denounced in this speech which was as violent as it was bitterly incendiary. Whipper's remarks, however, met with "no response [from Smalls' supporters] except from a few chronic offenders who stood around."[48]

On other occasions Smalls sounded like Whipper. At Edisto, both he and his supporters drew the color line. A black supporter, Butler Spears, stated that the fight in the district was "between the white men, who acted from self-interested motives, and the Negro." Once elected to office, white people in the district cared "no more for the people." He urged blacks to rally round their own man Robert Smalls. Smalls too added his own fire. Elliot

[48] Charleston *News and Courier,* October 22, 1884.

had accused him of being a convict and a bribe taker. "I have
never been inside of a prison's door," he told an enthusiastic
audience. He urged black people to vote solidly for him who
was not only black but had fought in the war that brought them
freedom while William Elliot "had fought with the Confererates
against them." Obviously anxious about the impact of Smalls'
stump speeches, the *News and Courier* editorialized that the Sea
Islanders were Smalls' "slaves." "Ignorant as they are on all
political subjects, having the facts perverted or hidden from them
by unscrupulous Republican office-seekers, and hearing as they
do only the Republican side of the story, is it any wonder the
easily-led, credulous and highly emotional colored man votes
for the party which he is told protects him from the oppression of
white Democrats?" The incendiary speeches of Smalls and his
supporters, the paper added, created "in the negro's heart a
feeling of distrust for those who are his best friends, and also
an overwhelming sense of his wrongs, imaginary though they
may be." The only way in which the influence of "these stirrers
up of strife and discord can be abated," concluded the paper,
was "for the Democrats to take the stump and expose their mis-
representations." Apparently, the *News and Courier* did not
understand the political magic of the "Gullah statesmen"—his
popularity with his people and his ability to personify their sufferings and declining political power.[49]

As election day approached, Smalls and his supporters adopted
even a stronger line. His campaign tours were enlivened by a
large retinue of Beaufort blacks and torch-carrying processions
led by the Beaufort brass band. More often than not, open-air
meetings were held. Blacks were advised to brave the opposition
of the Democrats and be around the polls on election day. "If
Col. Elliot is counted in, and Smalls counted out," Whipper told
an audience, "we will raise hell with the whites down here." The
chairman of the Colleton County Republicans, a black named
Paul, advised his constituents to "kill the damned white man
whenever the opportunity offers." The pulpits of black churches
were turned into campaign stands where blacks were urged to

[49] *Ibid.,* October 25, 1884.

"fight for their rights." As the Democrats were reported perfect-
ing a plan to negate the wishes of the people, Beaufort blacks
bought large quantities of arms and prepared for a showdown.
The Democrats were equally determined and it was widely believed that "there would be trouble." Both sides openly declared
that "forbearance has ceased to be a virtue."[50]

Fortunately, the election came off with minimum trouble. The
blacks responded to the appeals by Smalls and he received a 4000-
vote majority, his largest since 1876. Once more, the Sea Islanders
had demonstrated their confidence in their leader. In the burst
of enthusiasm that followed, black representatives in the state
legislature put up Smalls' name for the United States Senate.
Nobody expected Smalls to win, and Wade Hampton, the Democratic candidate, received thirty-one votes to three for Smalls.[51]

Probably realizing that this might be his last chance, Smalls
did his best work in the Forty-ninth Congress. He was appointed
to the War Claims Committee and submitted fifteen war claims
to that body. He presented eight private claims, introduced thir-
teen private bills and seven public ones, and proposed amendments to two pending bills—all in the first session! Significantly
too, and in keeping with his traditional concern for his district,
many of these bills dealt with needed improvements at Beaufort.
One provided for the redemption and sale of some farm lands in
Beaufort County still held by the Federal Government. Another
asked for the restoration to the town of Beaufort of the books,
maps, and pamphlets removed by the Federal soldiers during the
late war. Still another called for the relief of the Beaufort
Mounted Guards. In another bill, Smalls called for the construction of a telegraph line from Georgetown, South Carolina, to
South Island and Wavery Mills, South Carolina, and for the display of storm and weather signals at these points.[52]

Smalls delivered two important prepared speeches in this Congress. One dealt with a pension voted by the House but vetoed
by President Cleveland for the widow of former Union general,

[50] *Ibid.*, November 3, 4, 1884.
[51] *Ibid.*, November 28, December 10, 1884.
[52] *Congressional Record*, 49th Congress, 1st Session, 481, 538, 1218, 1365,
1919, 3401, 4046, 4860.

David Hunter. Smalls had introduced the bill in the House, and because of the "peculiar relations he bore to that distinguished soldier and patriot for whose widow the bill provided," he decided to defend it.

He would be doing injustice to himself, his constituency, and his race, if he failed to state why he had introduced the bill, Smalls declared. He had asked for the pension without Mrs. Hunter's knowledge and not "so much because of the necessities of their condition but as the grateful tribute of a country saved by their heroism and valor." He denounced the President's veto as an "ungracious and unpatriotic act" because the bill was "the nation's tribute to heroic deed." Hunter was "the country's pride while living," and it was "just that his bereaved widow should be the nation's ward." The pittance of fifty dollars per month which he had called for, Smalls admitted, was more than would have been allowed by existing law, but it fell "far short of the proper estimate of the eminent services rendered by General Hunter during a long, eventful, and illustrous career." To him and his race, the circumstances surrounding the Hunter case were "singularly exceptional." For less than a quarter of a century theretofore, black people were "hewers of wood and drawers of water," their importance consisting largely "in their money value." Then came the war and General Hunter. "The convulsion aroused our minds to active thought and operation," he passionately declared, "and bade us hope for a more useful and grander experience in the affairs of life. We heard the words of hope amid the din of battle and the clash of arms. We began to realize that we were human beings." General Hunter was part and parcel of that "band of angels" that lifted the black man's life which hitherto had been "one long eternal night, not even an occasional silver lining in the sky to bid hope for a brighter future or a happier day" into the bright sunshine of freedom. He added: "We are not an ungrateful nor unappreciative people, Mr. Speaker. We cannot forget the Moses who led us out of the land of bondage."[53]

53 *Ibid.,* Appendix, 319-320.

General Hunter's order of May 9, 1862, declaring the slaves in the states of Georgia, Florida, and South Carolina "for ever free," became, to the blacks, a lasting testimony to Hunter's concern for black people. After those "immortal words" were spoken, "then and there freedom unfurled her standard to the air. A new inspiration was imparted to us; a new heaven was opened to our vision." Both Generals Hunter and Frémont, who had taken a similar action in behalf of the freedmen, were, Smalls declared, "freedom's pioneers; and so far advanced were they that their proclamations failed to command the approval of freedom's martyred President."

To this official testimony of General Hunter's concern for black people, Smalls added a catalogue of "acts of personal beneficence and kindness practiced by General Hunter toward the down-trodden race"—his relief of the needy, his education of the ignorant, and his encouragement of the oppressed. He alleged that it was because of Hunter's connection with the freedmen and his public hostility toward "the late rebels" that the President had vetoed the bill. Other members who were not personally acquainted with Hunter might not appreciate what he meant to black people. For Smalls personally, it was Hunter who had sent him to Washington to meet President Lincoln and thus make possible the enlistment of Port Royal "contrabands" into the Union army. He passionately concluded:

> Mr. Speaker, by the variations and methods of modern politics, my race of upward seven millions of people are represented on this floor by the honorable gentleman from North Carolina and myself. How long this injustice will be tolerated I will not dare to prophesy; but so long as one of us be permitted on this floor our voice and vote will not be withheld from any measure of legislation which will add to the prosperity and happiness of all the people, without regard to color or condition, and the permanence and greatness of a common country.[54]

The second speech dealt with his joint resolution for the relief of sufferers in the lower counties of his state from a flood which had destroyed crops and rendered a large number of citizens

54 *Ibid.*

homeless. Smalls indicated that immediate relief was necessary to prevent impending starvation. The prospects of aid from the state legislature were slim because that body would not meet until the following November. Smalls admitted that actually such relief was the province of the state, but he cited instances of aid to Portland, Oregon, and Memphis in similar critical times. The Congress should leave aside "argument or hair-splitting constitutional disquisition," Smalls added, and "in view of the emergency whose delay is death," should act immediately. As with many of his legislative endeavors in this Congress, Smalls failed in this effort. Constitutionality and legality prevailed over an awareness of human suffering as speakers who argued that such relief was a prerogative of the state prevailed over those who would put humanity above legality.[55]

In this session, too, Smalls supported the spoilsman in their opposition of civil service reform. Since the 1870's the Republican party had been attacked for an uninhibited use of the spoils system which made the civil service, according to its opponents, "a mere instrument of partisan tyranny and personal ambition . . . an object of selfish greed . . . a scandal and reproach upon free institutions." Abolition of the system, the opponents contended, would make honesty, capacity, and fidelity the only claims to public office and free government workers from favoritism and patronage. Smalls, who relied heavily on patronage to keep supporters in line and was irreconcilably opposed to anything sponsored by the Democrats irrespective of merit, joined his Republican colleagues in a successful opposition to civil service reform. He also voted for the repeal of the 1867 Tenure of Office Act which attempted to limit the President's authority to dismiss cabinet members.[56]

Smalls made his last race in 1886. To the South Carolina whites he was the last symbol of their painful past. Thus, both the national and state Democratic administrations combined to remove this thorn in their flesh. Governor Richardson called for unity and harmony within the state Democratic ranks so that

55 *Ibid.*, 330-331.
56 *Ibid.*, 2226, 2675, 2696, 2700.

all forces would be directed against the black oasis in white South Carolina. "Division in our ranks," he told an enthusiastic audience at Florence, "means defeat. No general can afford to divide his forces in the presence of the enemy. Division with us means rack and ruin." He reminded his listeners that with Smalls and his supporters still in the political arena, "there was danger in the future," and urged every lover of the state to "work to remove this danger." From Washington, Senator Hampton brought word that President Cleveland was "personally interested" in the defeat of Smalls. Representative Samuel Dibble, in charge of the Democratic Congressional Committee in South Carolina, was directed to give "special attention to the Seventh District." Back in South Carolina he confidently predicted the "end of Smalls," and declared that a strong effort would be made to send "a solid Democratic delegation to the Fiftieth Congress."[57]

Against these powerful forces Smalls resolved to wage another strenuous campaign. The factional fight within the local Republican party compounded his problems. He was making "a desperate struggle to secure re-election," Dibble indicated in a letter to the Baltimore *Sun,* but the confidence which the Republicans of that section once reposed in Smalls had been shaken. The black vote was said to be "pretty well divided," and some blacks were reported ready to vote for William Elliot, the Democratic candidate. On some occasions Smalls tried to stem the swelling tide of Democratic appeal to the black voters by speaking flatteringly of the then Democratic administration. But it was to no avail. The Democrats had decided that the time had "arrived for the redemption of the black district from Republican control."[58]

As the campaign wore on, a peculiar color line developed. The problem of maintaining harmony between the "pure blacks" and "the yellow and neutral tints" had reared its head in earlier elections, but Smalls had assumed that, since the Democrats could not put up a candidate in the district, there was no need

[57] Charleston *News and Courier,* October 16, 1886.
[58] *Ibid.,* quoting the *Sun.*

to "pander to the loud-mouthed, blatant strikers of black com-
plexion in the party." This time, however, things were different.
The Democrats were prepared to exploit the situation because it
would be to the detriment of Smalls. The "pure blacks," of
whom Smalls was not one, consisted mainly of the rice and
cotton plantation workers who were in the majority in the district. At a convention at Beaufort on October 15, the "darker
shades" indicated their dissatisfaction with Smalls and accused
him of favoring the lighter Negroes for office. Actually, Smalls'
stand at the convention would tend to indicate that he did not
regard "shades" as an important factor in selecting officers. He
pleaded for harmony and indicated that it would be to the interest of the district "to select men for the legislature who could
read and write and had some attainments derived from travel
or as waiters." Unfortunately, however, the darker citizens were
usually not among the better educated, and they could be led to
believe that Smalls' recommendations were designed to exclude
them from office-holding. The convention thus broke up in a
riot, leaving the predominantly "darker delegation" from St.
Helena Island "the most dissatisfied." They swore vengeance on
Smalls, told him not "to come to the island again," declared
their intention never to let him speak there, and vowed to support Elliott, the Democratic candidate, in the election.[59]

Given these developments and the combined determination of
the Democrats, there was little doubt that Smalls would be defeated. His largest support in previous elections had come from
St. Helena where there were almost one thousand voters. As
election day approached, the News and Courier reported that
Smalls was "undoubtedly uneasy" and saw his chances "getting
smaller and beautifully less." But the Democrats were still not
confident of victory in the "Black District," and still resorted to
all kinds of fraud and intimidation. The official returns showed
Elliot the victor by a safe vote. On Elliot's victory, the Greenville News said:

Our side may, and doubtless will, prove that the county boards
acted within the law in throwing out many boxes and hundreds of

[59] Ibid., October 18, 1886.

votes for irregularities, but the fact will stand out bold and unquestioned that Smalls has been defeated by the official negligence of Democratic authority. . . . The state will be put before the country as being party to a plain deliberate and wanton fraud.[60]

Henry Cabot Lodge sponsored Smalls' contest in the Fiftieth Congress, and Smalls was allowed to speak in his own behalf. He denounced the testimony of Democrats who had justified his defeat as a "competitive examination in falsehood," denied charges of bribery and corruption in connection with his indictment in 1877, and insisted that his popularity with his people had not declined:

> They tell you that my vote has fallen off, that my people have gone against me. . . . No, Sir, no vote has fallen off. The vote is the same today and more, but the Democrats have improved their methods of preventing votes from getting into the box.[61]

The national mood, however, was no different from that of the white people of South Carolina, and the House refused to seat Smalls. Commenting on the decision of the Congress, one contemporary called it a "foul blot upon the escutcheons of the civilized white pagans of the South whose plans miscarried in the '60's' as they will in '88.' " In 1888, however, Smalls was persuaded to retire in favor of a younger candidate, Thomas Miller. Thus ended the congressional career of the "King of Beaufort."

In assessing the activities of Smalls in Congress, some historians have relied heavily on an opinion expressed by a Negro newspaper, the New York *Enterprise,* immediately after Smalls' defeat in the 1886 race:

> There is not a single instance in his political history as a member of Congress where he has ever put forth a measure to promote the interest of his race. . . . He was more of a target of ridicule than a statesman. . . . He has only retained his place so long because though ignorant himself, he was just smart enough to gain the support and

[60] *Ibid.,* also November 9, 1886 and November 24, 1886 quoting the *Greenville News.*

[61] Speech of Hon. Robert Smalls in the House of Representatives, Pamphlet, Moorland Foundation, Howard University Library.

confidence of the black voters in his district by his outward seeming
and flattery.[62]

Clearly, however, this opinion was not justified by the facts.
Smalls had dedicated his whole life to the interest of the black
man in his district and the nation at large. His partisan support
of everything Republican and opposition to almost everything
Democratic during his terms in Congress were largely because of
his firm belief that Republicanism was the vehicle for the salvation of the black people. This was natural enough when the chief
concern of Southern Democrats in these years was the elimination of the black man's vote and influence. It is true that Smalls
did not often succeed in winning over Congress to adopt his
proposals, but this was more a commentary on the times than
on Smalls' effectiveness and ability. That he tried so much in
the face of the overwhelming power and influence of the opposition was a tribute to his courage and tenacity. Undismayed by
the seemingly hopeless situations, he was always ready to take a
firm stand against the forces that were reducing the blacks from
political power in the Reconstruction years to a political cipher
in "redeemed" South Carolina. From Washington, the arena for
the battle for freedom, as Smalls would call it, shifted once more
back to his native South Carolina.

[62] Charleston *News and Courier*, November 9, 1886, quoting the *Enterprise*.

VI

FOR AN EQUAL CHANCE IN THE
BATTLE OF LIFE

WHEN ROBERT SMALLS left the nation's capital to return to South Carolina the hopes of equality for blacks which he had had during the Civil War and Radical Reconstruction yielded to frustration and anxiety. Radical Reconstruction which had attempted to bring them into the mainstream of American life then seemed to many whites to have been a frightful scourge and a crime, its painful memories to be forgotten in the interest of sectional harmony and national reconciliation. The sectional hatreds from which the blacks had profited now seemed not only obsolescent but unprofitable within the context of the changing economic situation which was carrying both North and South into the industrial world. It was a world for which the contemporary historian, A. B. Hart, found black people ill-prepared, "it being undeniable that the Negro has no such spirit of acquisition, no such willingness to sacrifice present delight for future good." The intellectual climate of the times, firmly rooted in the doctrine of social Darwinism and the "white man's burden," also lent support to the national posture. In this atmosphere, weariness overtook the former spirit of reform, and even prominent friends like Thomas Higginson and Carl Shurz abandoned the cause for which they had so nobly stood. Deserted by these friends and soon to be dismayed by the death of Frederick Douglass, their "uncrowned king" who apparently left no heir, the black people might well have resigned themselves to the evolving cycle of frustration and betrayal.[1]

Meanwhile, many South Carolina whites were becoming impatient of the pace toward total elimination of black political power and the return of black people to their "natural" position on the "evolutionary ladder." Increasingly, violence became an accepted way of accomplishing this.[2] "A disregard for inflicting pain and shedding blood became lamentably common." Any act of murder of a black man became something to be admired rather than condemned. This, Governor W. D. Simpson maintained, was "one of the greatest evils left in the tract of the Civil War."[3] White mobs which lynched blacks received praises from the white populace. For, the editor of the *Daily Register* argued, "Judge Lynch is an abler judge and a more humane man and a truer discerner of equality than many who have figured as justices in our reconstructed and semi-barbarous era." The *News and Courier* had opposed violence as a means of "redemption" but now sanctioned it and argued that "it will be a woeful day for South Carolina when crimes of a particular class are punished, if punished at all, after long imprisonment, a tedious trial and the procrastination which lawyers practice on behalf of their clients." When two blacks accused of rape and murder were lynched in 1881, the same paper saw the white mob as representing "society at large," and as "exponents of a law that is older

---

[1] A. B. Hart, *The Southern South* (New York, 1910), 132, 149. For a discussion of the situation in the late nineteenth century, see the following: John Higham, *Strangers in the Land* (New Brunswick, 1955) , Chaps. 4-6 where he describes the national xenophobic mania; C. Vann Woodward, *The Origins of the New South* (Baton Rouge, 1951); Paul H. Buck, *The Road to Reunion* (Boston, 1937), 294-297.

[2] The celebrated Cash-Shannon duel of 1882 is often taken as marking the turning point in the change of tactics. Wallace, *History of South Carolina*, III, 330-332.

[3] "A South Carolinian," *Atlantic Monthly*, XXXIX (April 1887), 468; *Journal of the Senate of the State of South Carolina, 1879-1880* (Columbia, S.C., 1880), 12; Tindall, *South Carolina Negroes*, 233-259.

than governments, and more venerable than the constitution of states."[4]

With such public approval the number of lynchings increased in the state. Between 1882 and 1890, there were no less than thirty, the best known being that in Barnwell in December 1889 in which eight blacks were killed, and the lynching of Willie Leaphart in 1890.[5] Though generally treated as punishment for crimes like rape, murder, and robbery, lynching might more properly be viewed as an instrument for the re-establishment of white supremacy in the state. Many of the lynchings took place in areas still under black control, and, significantly, there were fewer lynchings in the years after the complete elimination of black political power in the state.[6]

In this "context of violence," some blacks sought refuge in migration. In 1879, a black convention at Nashville, Tennessee, at which South Carolina was represented, called on blacks to migrate to states where they could still enjoy "all the rights guaranteed by the laws and constitution of the United States." Between 1879 and 1881, a sizable number left South Carolina for Kansas.[7] The pace quickened with rising violence, and between December 24 and 31, 1881, an estimated five thousand blacks left "bloody Edgefield." They complained that they could not vote at elections; that, if they voted, their ballots were not counted; that life was insecure and dangerous.

> For ten years we have tried to make money and have not been able to do so. We are poorer now than when we began, we have less, in fact, we have nothing. . . . There is no use trying to get along under the old conditions any longer, and we have just determined to go somewhere and take a new start.[8]

[4] Columbia *Daily Register,* May 28 and June 2, 1882; Charleston *News and Courier,* January 20, 1881.
[5] N.A.A.C.P., *Thirty Years of Lynching in the United States, 1889-1910* (New York, 1919), 88-91; Charleston *News and Courier,* December 29, 30, 1889 and May 6, 7, 14, 1890 for the Willie Peaphart and Barnwell incidents.
[6] See Tindall, *South Carolina Negroes,* 239 for a similar point of view.
[7] Columbia *Daily Register,* December 23, January 8, 1881.
[8] Charleston *News and Courier,* January 2, 1882.

Spurred on by various organizations which sprang up to appeal for migrants from the state, and impressed by glowing accounts of the "promised land" painted by such groups, many blacks left the state.[9]

Black leaders were divided in their reaction to migrations from the state. Former Congressman Joseph Rainey saw it as the only escape from the outrages perpetrated against them. Bishop William Arnett of the African Methodist Episcopal Church urged blacks to go with their families and promised a pioneer's reward to those who responded to his plea.[10]

Robert Smalls was among the leaders who opposed emigration. He would support movement from communities where racial antagonism rendered peaceful co-existence with whites impossible to areas of relative calm within the state. He invited those in other counties to move to Beaufort where it was "hardly probable that any prisoner will ever be taken from jail by a white mob and lynched, let his color or offense be what it may." A white reporter in Beaufort suspected that Smalls was exploiting the migratory surge for his own political advantage. Even if this was true, Smalls was quite correct. The "Black District" did hold a better promise for blacks. In fact, Beaufort became a refuge for many Negroes from Hampton and Colleton counties. Some 1500 moved into Beaufort between 1878 and 1879, with more coming in succeeding years.[11]

For blacks who remained in the state, perhaps the most important issue in these years was the movement which represented both agrarian discontent and Negrophobia, variously called the "Reform" or Tillman Movement. From 1876 to 1895, black suffrage remained basic to all political issues in the state. In 1881,

[9] Report of the Industrial Commission on Agricultural Labor, *House Report*, 57th Congress, 1st Session, 819, describes the work of the organizations. One advertisement described Arkansas as "a tropical country of soft and balmy air, where cocoanuts, oranges, lemons, bananas grew." Cited in Tindall, *South Carolina Negroes*, 174.

[10] J. C. Galloway Scrapbook, Moorland Foundation, Howard University; Benjamin W. Arnett, *Annual Address Delivered Before the Faculty, Students, and Friends of Claflin University* (Columbia, S.C., 1889), 32.

[11] Columbia *Daily Register*, January 10, 1882; Charleston *News and Courier*, February 2, 1890; *Appleton's Annual Cyclopaedia*, IV (1879), 813.

Edward McCrady, historian of the state and a Conservative legislator from Charleston, advocated "raising the standard of citizenship" to insure a political class of intelligent and propertied
white and black men.[12] The McCrady program proved unpopu-
lar with both poor whites and some blacks. Black leader Thomas
Miller denounced it as a trap to keep "the middle classes of poor
whites, together with negroes, from having anything to do with
the elections." He argued that the program actually represented
an attempt by the upper-class whites to provide "an opportunity
for rings and fossils to retain power." All chances of an alliance
between the poor whites and the blacks floundered, however, on
the rocks of economic competition and the poor white Negrophobia which had been cultivated since the 1870's. Frightened
by the increasing indications of a political rapport between the
upper class whites and the blacks and the possibility of the
former using the black vote to stifle their program for radical
economic reform, the poorer whites united to capture the Democratic party in 1890 when their leader, Ben Tillman, best remembered as Pitchfork Ben, won the gubernatorial election.[13]

From the beginning, because of a belief in the innate inferiority of blacks, a pathological fear of black rule, and the necessity of competing with blacks for the few crumbs the depressed
agriculture of the state had to offer, the Tillmanites had seen
disfranchisement of blacks as one solution to their political and
economic ills. This became particularly obvious after the 1888
election when the Conservative Democrats openly courted the
black voters. In his Shell Manifesto opening his campaign in
1890, Tillman called for a constitutional convention "that we
may have an organic law formed by South Carolinians and
suited to our wants, thereby lessening the burdens of taxation
and giving us better government." Such a constitution would
place restrictions upon the social and political rights of blacks.
Though he failed to win enough support for the convention in
his first term as governor, Tillman got enough support in his

12 *The Necessity for Raising the Standard of Citizenship* (Charleston, 1881),
38; *The Registration of Electors* (Charleston, 1881), 3-5.
13 Columbia *Daily Register*, December 3, 1881; Simkins, *The Tillman
Movement in South Carolina* (Durham, 1926), 103-134 for details.

second term to get the Assembly to call for a vote on a convention in the 1894 election. This would be the most important
issue in that campaign.[14]

Though not too enthusiastic about preserving the black vote,
the Conservative Democrats were bitterly opposed to the holding
of any convention, which, in any case, would be dominated by
the Tillmanites. The Tillman-controlled legislature would make
the laws providing for the election of delegates to the convention
and could use their power and influence to keep out opponents
of the Tillman Ring. Moreover, they reasoned, given the public
utterances of Tillman, such a convention would endanger the
political rights of both black and white people. Summing up
their case, the *Sun* declared that "the Negro Rule Scare" used
by the Tillmanites was extremely overdrawn and used "to the
injustice and suppression of the great majority of our people."
The *Courier* warned of the danger in the lack of provision for
the proposed constitution to be submitted to the people for
ratification. "The advocates of the new constitution do not dare
to trust it to the people," the paper declared, "the people must
decide whether they dare to trust it to its advocates."[15]

The Tillmanites drummed up support for their cause by in-
voking the specter of black rule and a possible return to the
days before 1876. The potential black voting population of
the state, they argued, was about forty thousand more than the
white. A fusion between Conservative Democrats, Independents,
and the blacks, which had almost happened in 1888, and was
now coalescing behind the opposing candidate for governor,
Sampson Pope, would result in the triumph of that faction.
Since the blacks would constitute the majority in such an alliance, this would mean a return to the days of black rule with
all their horror and humiliation for the "superior race." Fortunately, an opportunity was being offered to the white people of
the state in the following convention to "obviate all future dan-

14 Charleston *News and Courier*, January 23, 1890; Columbia *Daily Register*,
October 31, 1894; *Journal of the General Assembly of the State of South
Carolina*, 1892 (Columbia, S.C., 1893), 418.

15 *Ibid.*, October 20 and 11, 1894 quoting the Charleston *Sun*; Columbia
State, September 28, 1894; also October 19, 1894.

ger, and fortify Anglo-Saxon civilization against every assault
from within and without." Tillman would not reveal his specific
plans for reducing the black vote. "That's my secret," he told an
audience. "Let the people of the state trust me. Let them vote
for the convention. The time to discuss the method for reducing
the negro majority is after the convention has been called." The
people should remember, however, that those opposed to holding
a convention were men "who want to put you back in the
caldron of hell from which you emerged in 1876."[16]

As the campaign progressed, black leaders in the state were increasingly drawn toward the much milder program of the Conservative-Independent coalition. Broadening the scope of their
appeals to include whites, they warned that "the very life of
suffrage in this state is at stake and other cherished rights and
interests are imperiled." A group of black ministers called on all
people to organize to stop this robbery of black political rights.
"The sugar-coated pledges made by Hampton in 1876 were
broken," they declared, and the constitutional convention would
be the climax in the process. Another group of blacks met in
Columbia and called for "cooperation with that class of white
men whom we know to be too proud, broad and humane to take
advantage of the weak." A Negro Ministerial Union issued a call
to the national government to intervene to stop this negation of
the "political rights of a majority by a small desperate minority."[17]

Meanwhile, Robert Smalls, a political foe of Tillman since the
congressional contests, was mapping out his own strategy. In the
election of 1890, Smalls had called upon the Sea Islanders to
support Alexander Haskell, a moderate Democrat ("though he
felt it repugnant to his feelings as a Republican to advise his
people to vote for any Democrat"), hoping thereby to "bring
about the defeat of this arch-enemy of my race."[18] In the 1894
election he gravitated toward the Conservative-Independent coa-

16 Columbia *Daily Register,* October 10, 28, and 30, 1894.
17 Columbia *Daily Register,* January 5 and 20, 1895; Columbia *State,* February 1, July 11, 1895; Yorkville *Enquirer,* January 23, 1893.
18 Robert Smalls, "Election Methods in South Carolina," *North American
Review,* CLI (November 1890), 599.

lition, whose program, though it represented no positive movement to protect black political rights, was less hostile than that
of the Tillmanites. Perhaps echoing Smalls' view, his son-in-law
and editor of the Beaufort *New South*, S. J. Bamfield, reminded
his readers of the imminent danger posed by the Tillmanites.
Unless some prompt action was taken, "these white supremacy
howlers will succeed in fastening upon the people an oligarchy
of fraud that will keep the [Tillman] Machine in power and the
honest people of the state under their heels for the next half
century." There was a "conspiracy against the purity of the
ballot box," he warned, and a "determination to continue the
system of fraudulent elections that have disgraced South Carolina
for so many years and brought reproach upon the people of the
state." On his own, Smalls tried to use his political connections
to influence the Conservatives to nominate candidates who were
acceptable to the black Republicans.[19]

Neither the black thrust nor the combined opposition of Independents and Conservative Democrats could stop the Tillmanites, however. In a campaign reminiscent of 1876, except that
this time cheating and violence were directed as much against
whites as blacks, the Tillmanites won the gubernatorial race as
well as the right to hold the convention. The *News and Courier*,
headlining the election news A MACHINE ELECTION—WHITE MEN
CHEAT WHITE MEN IN SOUTH CAROLINA, carried accounts of fraud
in several counties. The defeated candidate for governor credited
the Tillmanite victory to "fraud of the blackest character." These
charges amounted to nothing, however, because neither the Tillman-controlled courts nor the legislature would act upon them.[20]

Having failed in their bid to stop Tillman from holding his
convention, Smalls and his black colleagues decided to alert the
nation. In an appeal to the New York *World* signed by Smalls,
Thomas Miller, R. B. Anderson, and Isaiah Reed, the black leaders drew attention to the impending action of the Tillmanites
which "ought to stir the conscience of the world." The conven-

19 Beaufort *New South*, March 7, 1895; Columbia *Daily Register*, September
27, 1894.
20 Charleston *News and Courier*, November 7, 10, 11, 12, 1894; Columbia
State, November 9, 1894.

tion had been called to disfranchise their race and would take such action as would paralyze the meager educational progress their people were making. The issue was racial, not political, they argued. For, there could be no doubt "that if Negroes of the state were to become Democrats, the white would become Republicans." They added that the blacks had never in fact been a threat to white supremacy because "even in the days of Republican ascendancy all the great offices, and a majority of all the offices, were held by white men, and no one ever thought of making that a Negro government." The plea fell on deaf ears, however, as the national audience was in no mood to listen.[21]

The convention which met in 1895 was very different both in intent and personnel from that of 1868. The latter had been called for the special purpose of giving the blacks political rights consonant with their status as citizens; that of 1895 met for the expressed purpose of taking those rights away. In 1868, there were 76 blacks to 48 whites; in 1895 there were only 6 blacks (all except one from Beaufort) to 154 whites (112 Tillmanites and 42 Conservatives). Most of the white delegates at the 1868 convention were sympathetic to the black cause; the white delegates at the 1895 convention were either avowed black haters or at least ambivalent in their attitudes. One of the rare common denominators to both conventions was the presence of two black veteran politicians—Robert Smalls and W. J. Whipper. In 1868 they helped draw guidelines for "an intelligent government faithful to the interests and liberties of the people." In 1895 they were there to see the same guidelines not only discredited but also overturned.[22]

The speech of Robert Aldrich, who was appointed temporary

[21] New York *World*, September 30, October 1, and November 7, 1895.
[22] See *Constitutional Convention Journal*, 1895, 3-8 for a list of the delegates. The following studies deal with the convention in greater detail: David D. Wallace, *The South Carolina Constitutional Convention of 1895*. Bulletin of the University of South Carolina, No. 197 (February 15, 1929); Tindall, "The Question of Race in the South Carolina Constitutional Convention of 1895," *Journal of Negro History*, XXXVII (July 1952), 277-303; "The Campaign for the Disfranchisement of Negroes in South Carolina," *Journal of Southern History*, XV (May 1949), 212-234; Simkins, *Pitchfork Ben Tillman*, 285-309 deals with the role of Tillman in the convention.

chairman of the convention, left no doubt what direction the deliberations would take. Declaring the gathering "the most important deliberative body that has assembled in South Carolina for a century," he urged a return to the constitution of 1790, "the only constitution South Carolina ever had and which was the work of her sovereign hands." The constitutions drawn in 1860 and 1865, he continued, were not representative; the former was designed to meet an emergency situation, the latter imposed on the state by the President of the nation. As for the constitution of 1868, it was illegal, being the "fruit of the Reconstruction Acts, which were notoriously unconstitutional." Besides, it was framed by "aliens, negroes and natives without character, all enemies of South Carolina, and was designed to degrade our state, insult our people and overturn our civilization." It was incumbent on the people now that they had regained control to do away with "that instrument of their humiliation in their day of defeat." In framing the new constitution the delegates should remember the principles of their forefathers who had framed the constitution of 1790. For, "we are not wiser in our day and generation than the children of light; and we will make no mistake in walking in the footsteps of our fathers." A return to the days of 1790, of course, meant a return to Anglo-Saxon supremacy.[23]

Since the disfranchisement of blacks was the major objective of the convention, the Committee on the Rights of Suffrage was the most important standing committee of the convention. Appointed on the second day of deliberations, the committee included eight Tillmanites and three Conservatives, and, above all, Ben Tillman as its chairman. It took suggestions from delegates, and received testimony and various proposals from several people. From these it drew up suffrage requirements, many of which were ultimately incorporated into the new constitution.

The suffrage articles of the new constitution forced each voter to run a gauntlet of numerous restrictions. Each prospective voter had to be a free man, twenty years of age, not a pauper

---

[23] *Constitutional Convention Journal*, 1895, 1-2; also 9-13 for a very similar speech by Governor Gary Evans.

nor a commissioned officer or private soldier, or a seaman or marine of the national navy. He must have resided in the state for at least two years, and in a county in which he wanted to vote six months before any election. He must be able to read and write the English language. Alternatively, he must have property valued at three hundred dollars or more, or be able to "understand" the constitution when read aloud. Every election manager was given the right to require of every elector proof of payment of all taxes assessed against him the previous year. In addition any person guilty of the following crimes could be disfranchised: burglary, arson, theft, perjury, treason, bigamy, forgery, robbery, adultery, wife-beating, house-breaking, breach of trust with fraudulent intent, fornication, incest, assault with intent to ravish, and miscegenation.[24]

The black vote was the main target of these provisions. While the literacy test would have affected many poor whites as well as blacks, the understanding clause provided a loophole for the former. In a letter to the New York *World,* Robert Smalls and the other black delegates interpreted the understanding clause in this way. Tillman would not accept a straight literacy qualification, they maintained, because this would mostly affect his own supporters. While blacks over twenty-one then outnumbered whites 132,949 to 102,657, the number of literate whites to blacks stood at 89,415 to 74,851. They estimated that though the Tillmanites outnumbered the Conservative whites by 60,000 to 35,000, disfranchisement of illiterate whites would reduce their majority to only 1200. In this event, a combined force of literate blacks and Conservative whites, more conjectural than real, could carry any election. It was to prevent this possibility that the Tillmanites inserted the understanding clause which could be used for indiscriminate enfranchisement of the poor whites.[25] The residential requirements could also result in the disfranchisement of many blacks because of their migratory habits. The payment of the poll tax in May, a time when ready cash was least

24 *Ibid.,* 42-43, 101-102, 111-122, 127-128 contain the various proposals made to the committee. For the final draft see *Constitution of 1895,* Article 11, Sections 3, 4, 6.
25 New York *World* cited by the Columbia *Daily Register,* October 4, 1895.

available to farmers and their mainly black dependents, was also a useful weapon against the black vote. The disfranchising crimes were supposed to be those most often committed by blacks. Thus, ambiguity in phraseology merely disguised the fact that the black vote was the target of all the suffrage provisions. In one of his franker moments, Tillman himself declared that "we are like an ostrich, hiding its head in the sand thinking we are safe unless we put in the constitution a provision that will give the people the idea that we are going to have fairness." The threat of Federal intervnetion was not completely dead.[26]

This clever attempt to disfranchise their race drew eloquent protest from the six black delegates. Thomas Miller opened by reminding the convention of the heroism and significant sacrifice and contributions of blacks to the national cause. He blamed the humiliation inflicted on the South during the Civil War not on the blacks, but on the "love of power and supreme arrogance" of the whites. James Wigg called for a straight literacy test. "You charge the negro is too ignorant to be entrusted with the suffrage," he declared. "I answer that you have not, nor dare you, make a purely educational test of the right to vote." He declared the doctrine of the incompatibility of white and black interests, the stock-in-trade of the Tillmanites, "a political subterfuge, a fallacy so glaring in its inception, so insulting to Providence, so contrary to reason and the logic of history, that one can scarcely refrain from calling into question either the sanity or honesty of its advocates." W. J. Whipper, the other veteran of 1868, defended the constitution of 1868, "the best constitution the state had ever had," denied that a period of black rule ever existed in South Carolina, and called for racial harmony as existed in Beaufort where blacks and whites held office. R. B. Anderson, the only black delegate from Georgetown, described the suffrage provisions as a scheme "conceived in iniquity and born in sin.[27]

Perhaps the most effective of the black speeches was that made by Robert Smalls. Smalls would not apologize for the past of his

[26] Columbia *Daily Register,* November 9, 1895.
[27] Mary J. Miller, *The Suffrage Speeches by Negroes in the Constitutional Convention* (n.d.), 3-13; Columbia *State,* October 26 and 27, 1895; Columbia *Daily Register,* October 29, 1895.

race nor stress the close, friendly, and by implication, paternal
relations of blacks and whites.

> I was born and raised in South Carolina, and today I live on the
> very spot on which I was born, and I expect to remain here as long
> as the great God allows me to live, and will ask no one else to let
> me remain. I love the state as much as any member of this con-
> vention.[28]

He wondered why the whites would then disfranchise a race that
had been so true to them, serving "our masters faithfully, and
willingly, and as we were made to do." He reviewed the previous
attempts to negate the political rights of his people. He did not
care what qualifications were imposed for the franchise provided
they were "fair and honest." As presented to the convention,
however, the suffrage articles were fradulent both in intention
and execution. A violently anti-black politician had in fact confessed to one of his friends that blacks need not take the plea
of fairness by the Tillmanites seriously because it was meant to
fool the poor whites known as the "crackers." The suffrage plan
might fool the crackers, Smalls declared, but no one else was in
doubt about its essentially fradulent nature. He dared Tillman
to accept a straight literacy qualification which would disfranchise over fourteen thousand whites. He warned against the labor
difficulties the passage of the suffrage articles would create for
the state. Many blacks disfranchised and dispossessed would leave,
thus exacerbating the already precarious labor situation.[29]

So forceful was the appeal of the black delegation and so favorable the response from the Conservative members and the state
press that Tillman felt it necessary to deliver a full-dress reply.
In his speech, Tillman sought to justify the elimination of the
black vote. "The question of the suffrage and its wise regulation,"
was the sole cause of calling the convention, he declared. Unre-
stricted use of the suffrage had led to the dark days of the Reconstruction period, an interregnum of almost unrelieved sordidness
in the life of the state. During those days, the black Republicans

[28] Sarah Smalls, ed., *Speeches by Robert Smalls at the Constitutional Convention* (Charleston, 1896), 6-9.
[29] Columbia *State,* October 27, 1895.

had drawn up a constitution which enabled them to fill the state house with "minions of Black Republicanism, officered and led by white thieves who came here for the expressed purpose of getting rich at the expense of our impoverished and fallen people." This period of black rule was marked by increase in public debt, mounting expenditures, increase in taxation, and, above all, fraud and corruption of the highest magnitude as evident from the extant documents in the state. Turning to the black delegates who were now making such a spirited and eloquent appeal in behalf of their race, Tillman declared that they featured prominently in "those years of good stealing in South Carolina." W. J. Whipper, "the ablest man of color" he had ever met, was also a bribe taker and swindler. Robert Smalls, according to the testimony before the Committee to Investigate Public Fraud, had been no less conspicuous in those years. How else, he asked, could the state prevent power from falling again into the hands of such public scoundrels apart from restricting the franchise.[30]

The following day Smalls made a speech in which he denied any connection with the fraud charged against him and dismissed Tillman's appeal as demagoguery. All the prosecution witnesses in the case against him were men of questionable and disreputable character; the charges were not proven; the whole thing was motivated by political vendetta rather than a strict concern for justice. Besides, Tillman had dragged the matter into the convention debates "to inflame the passions of the delegates against Republicans and force them to vote for this most infamous suffrage bill, which seeks to take away the right to vote from two thirds of the qualified voters of the state." Despite Tillman's diatribe on the black race, Smalls would not attempt to answer back:

My race needs no special defense for the past history of them in this country proves them to be the equal of any people anywhere. All they need is an equal chance in the battle of life.[31]

[30] *Constitutional Convention Journal*, 443-444, 446-472.
[31] *Ibid.*, 476; also see Chap. IV for the trial.

He had been honored by his race "with a seat on this floor," Smalls continued, and he intended to serve them to the best of his ability. Tillman's denunciations and attacks on him could not becloud his past record:

> I stand here the equal of any man. I started out in the war with the Confederates; they threatened to punish me and I left them. I went to the Union army. I fought in seventeen battles to make glorious and perpetuate the flag that some of you trampled under your feet. Innocent of every charge attempted to be made here to-day against me, no act of yours can in any way blur the record that I have made at home and abroad.[32]

Smalls' defense of his race and himself drew praise from the convention delegates, prominent black citizens in the nation, and some newspapers in the state. One white delegate from Darlington wondered "what oppressed people, denied the opportunity for the cultivation of good manners, the refining influences of civilization and religion," had ever sent a delegation anywhere who "in their deportment, in their powers of reasoning, in their rhetorical ability, in their knowledge of the laws of the land . . . could surpass in ability that colored delegation from Beaufort." The Sumter *Watchman and Southron,* taken aback by the denial of an educational qualification which the blacks asked for, wondered whether "all talk about the rule of the intelligent and superior race" was "buncombe." A dispatch from a black congregation in Philadelphia praised Smalls for the "dignity, courage, and singular ability" by which he had done "lasting honor to the Negro race and American patriotism." Another called Smalls' stand "a brilliant moral victory of parliamentary minority" which convincingly proved to the world the black man's right to ballot and showed beyond all doubt that "the fear of Negro domination is not born so much of regard for their numbers as for their intellectual ability. It is not Negro ignorance but Negro intelligence that is being feared."[33]

[32] *Ibid.*
[33] Miller, *Suffrage Speeches,* 3-4; New York *Press,* October 5, 1895 cited by Smalls, *Speeches,* 24-25.

However praiseworthy their efforts, the blacks proved power-
less in stopping the Tillmanites from carrying out their design.
Exasperated by the talk about fair elections, a fanatical Tillman
supporter declared that they wanted neither fair elections nor
educational qualifications because "we will get left at that every
time" and "the black man is learning to read faster than the
white man." The Tillmanites utilized their numerical superiority
to pass the suffrage articles by seventy-seven to forty-one votes.[34]

The preoccupation of the convention with black suffrage
brought the related questions of racial intermarriage and lynching to the fore. A resolution had been introduced to probibit
"the intermarriage of white persons with negroes, mulatoes or
persons of mixed blood descended from a negro or their living
together as man and wife." Though the resolution was unfavorably reported by the legislative committee, Smalls seized the opportunity to back the white delegates into a corner from which
he thought they could not escape. He introduced an amendment
to the effect that any white person found guilty of cohabiting
with a black should be barred from holding office. Moreover, the
child of such an affair should bear the name of its father and
inherit property as if he were legitimate. In support of his amendment, Smalls reminded the delegates that if a black man should
improperly approach a white woman, he would be hanged, and
"perhaps properly so." If, however, the convention should be
called upon to apply the same rule to white men who insulted
or debauched black women, it would "adjourn sine die for lack
of a quorum."[35]

Smalls' amendment threw the white delegates into consternation. "The coons had the dogs up the tree for a change," one
delegate commented on the white reaction, and "intended to
keep them there until they admit they are wrong." The *State*
argued that the whites had no choice but to swallow the dose
concocted by Smalls with the best possible grace they could
muster. Not entirely unsympathetic with Smalls' proposals, Ben

[34] Columbia *Daily Register,* November 2, 1895; *Constitutional Convention
Journal,* 1895, 517.
[35] *Constitutional Convention Journal,* 1895, 150; Columbia *State,* October
3, 1895.

Tillman introduced a substitute amendment to punish miscegenation as a crime. This, he argued, would "protect Negro women against debauchery of white men degrading themselves to the level of black women." Neither Tillman's substitute nor Smalls' original amendment passed the convention, however. The new constitution merely had a provision against intermarriage but prescribed no punishment for the guilty.[36]

Like his suffrage speech, Smalls' stand on miscegenation drew comments of approval from several quarters. In a telegram from Boston, dated October 16, 1895, black clergymen and laymen of the city congratulated Smalls for his stand for "virtue and chastity." The Christian churches "are with you in your struggle," they declared. Indeed, "the civilized world indorses the sentiment expressed by you. May God save the state of South Carolina from its barbarism."[37]

Closely related to the issue of miscegenation was the delicate question of defining a "Negro." The legislative committee described as Negro anybody with about one-eighth or more black blood. George Tillman, Ben's cousin, argued that this would embarrass certain families in his district who, though they had Negro blood, had furnished able soldiers to the Confederacy and were received in respectable society. He made the claim that in fact there was not one pure-blooded Caucasian on the floor of the convention! Accordingly, he pleaded for the retention of an 1879 law which defined as Negro those with more than one-fourth black blood. The convention, however, settled for the one-eighth provision reported by the legislative committee.[38]

Other important anti-black measures written into the organic law included the segregation of the state's educational institutions, public transportation, and other public places. The new labor law bound blacks to agriculture only. A strong anti-lynch law which might have protected blacks against white mobs was declared by one delegate to be "so extreme in its severity that it will defeat its own object, and . . . no conviction will ever be made under it." It was therefore rejected. The one success the

[36] *Ibid.*, October 4, 1895; *Constitution of 1895*, Article III, Section 33.
[37] Cited in Smalls, *Speeches*, 29.
[38] *Ibid.*, October 17, 1885.

black delegates scored was the provision to establish the Colored Normal, Agricultural, Industrial, and Mechanical College at Orangeburg.[39]

When the convention wound up its work, it had established the legal bases not only for the political disfranchisement of blacks, but also their reduction to the lowest rung of all aspects of life in the state. In order to get these laws, the state also sacrificed some of the modern and democratic reforms which were in their infancy in the state. An impulse toward home rule in local government foundered on the black majority. Otherwise beneficial education provisions were discarded because "the black man was learning to read faster than the white." Black drinking habits entered the discussion on liquor control, black ownership of dogs the debate on taxation. The creation of new counties which would have brought local government nearer to the people was dropped because of the distribution of the black population. These were the prizes the state had to pay for effecting Jim Crow.[40]

On the role of Robert Smalls in this all-important convention, one can, perhaps do no better than quote a contemporary assessment:

> Mr. Smalls was a potent factor in this convention and the ringing speeches made by him were masterpieces of impregnable logic, consecutive reasoning, biting sarcasm and fiery invective. His denunciation of mob violence and all forms of caste prejudice from political persecution to the provision for the intermarriage of the races surprised and shocked the negro-hating element of the South. His arguments were simply unanswerable, and the keenness of his wit, the cleverness of his arraignment, and the persistence with which he routed his opponents from one subterfuge to another astounded the convention, and showed its members that the negro's capacity for intelligence, courage and manhood was not inferior to the bluest blood in the old Palmetto State.[41]

Robert Smalls' opposition to the forces that threatened the political, social and economic well-being of his people did not

[39] *Constitutional Convention Journal,* 1895, 655-656, 577-580.

[40] See Tindall, "Question of Race," 303.

[41] Newspaper Clippings by Mrs. Hall in Miscellaneous Newspaper Clippings, Moorland Foundation, Howard University.

end at the convention. The organic law had been written, but Smalls considered it morally imperative for a man to resist and even negate bad laws through the use of constitutional channels. Apparently still trusting in the good sense of the American people, he undertook a national campaign to awaken the nation to the "unnecessary and cruel laws" in South Carolina. In the several appearances he made campaigning for William McKinley in the presidential election of 1896, he spoke out against the laws in the South in general and the South Carolina new constitution in particular. At Fort Scott, Kansas, he asserted that blacks who paid taxes on property valued at $12,500,000 in 1870 deserved better treatment. Even if administered fairly, he argued, the South Carolina suffrage provisions were a clear invitation to fraud and dishonesty purposely directed against the black man. At other places, he called on the "good people of America" to intervene to save the explosive situation in South Carolina.

A reported interview in which Senator Shelby M. Collom of Illinois was quoted as favoring a reduction in Southern congressional delegation now that many of its citizens had been disfranchised opened a new avenue of attack for Smalls. This should be treated as a matter "very near to the heart of every honest American citizen," Smalls declared in a letter to the senator. He detailed the vagaries of South Carolina registration and election laws and methods which in their conduct "Out Herod Herod." The understanding clause, the use of Democratic election commissioners and officers even in the black district, and "such other high-handed methods" had resulted in the disfranchisement of more than 10,000 blacks in South Carolina.[42]

It was his understanding, Smalls continued, that the next Congress would be considering the status of the people in the newly acquired possessions of Puerto Rico and the Philippines. "Does not charity begin at home?" Smalls asked. "Had not the American Republic first be just to their own citizens at home before they look after the welfare of the strangers without the gate?" He had contributed his utmost to the Republican triumph of 1896 in

[42] Robert Smalls, "Open Letter to Senator Cullom," Newspaper Clippings by Mrs. Hall, Miscellaneous Newspaper Clippings, Moorland Foundation, Howard University.

the hope that "the conscience of the nation may be awakened to the rights of which my people are deprived." During the last campaign, when he spoke against Democratic fradulent election practices in his state, the people of Fort Scott, Kansas, had indicated a desire to go along with whatever plans there were to remedy the situation. He knew the Senator would use "his good offices" to either work for the reduction of Southern representation or force the South to provide "an honest election law, by which every man who is entitled to vote under the Constitution of the United States as well as that of the state can cast his ballot unhampered and have the same counted." He was championing this course, he indicated, not out of revenge, but because "the present law is disgraceful and a menace to the republican form of government." He was aware that Senator Tillman, "whose sole stock in trade is to malign and mis-represent the status of my people," would do all he could to block all action in the Senate. But Senator Cullom should remember that he was from the "great state, a state which gave to this country (the greatest country on earth) in 1860 the immortal Lincoln." Moreover, the Senator needed not to be reminded that "a country founded on the principle of 'for the people and by the people' " could not "neglect the rights and interest of the ten millions or more of its own citizens at home on account of color." Above all the Senator had sworn to protect and defend the Constitution of the United States, and this included the Fourteenth and Fifteenth Amendments.

It was all to no avail, however. The Republican party and the nation in general were finding the race question increasingly politically unprofitable. In 1898 Representative Edgar D. Crumpacker, Republican of Indiana, introduced a resolution in Congress to initiate an inquiry into the justice and expediency of reducing Southern representation. A reduction of about 40 per cent in the South's representation in Congress and in the Electoral College was declared to be "just and logical." But, as a Washington correspondent put it, President McKinley would do nothing about this matter because action would be "bad politics." Perhaps if McKinley were re-elected, and if the Republicans won a majority in both houses of Congress, the time would seem ripe for "this great action."[43] With such an unfavorable national posture, Robert Smalls contended himself with organizing his electorate within the limits of the law and the people to defend themselves against lynching by white mobs. By 1903, a resident of Beaufort County reported that, although literate male blacks in that county outnumbered the white voters 3434 to 977, "the registration officials do not allow registered Negro voters to outnumber the whites."[44]

[43] R. W. Logan, *The Betrayal of the Negro* (New York, 1965), 217.
[44] Cited in Tindall, *South Carolina Negroes,* 88.

VII

THE LAST YEARS

ROBERT SMALLS did not spend the last years of his life brooding over disappointments and defeats. The futility of his stand against segregation and the elimination of black political power were discouraging, but Smalls had also won enough admiration and support from highly placed Republicans in Washington to ensure himself a share of the spoils of office in the years of Republican administration. Thus, until his death in 1915, Smalls remained in the public eye as the collector of customs for the Port of Beaufort, as an organizer for the black Republicans of his district, or as a prospective candidate for the United States Ambassadorship to Haiti or Liberia.[1]

While many blacks, disenchanted by the failures of the Republicans to protect their rights, had been deserting the party,[2] Robert Smalls had remained steadfast. In 1888 he attended the party's national convention and supported Benjamin Harrison, the party's presidential candidate. The collectorship of customs

---

[1] William Smalls indicated that his father's ability and worth were recognized by such congressional leaders as Mark Hanna, Henry Cabot Lodge, Robert La Follette, and John D. Long, Governor of Massachusetts. He credited the fact that his father's appointments to Federal offices were always confirmed without reference to any committee to the respect these people had for him.

[2] For details see Logan, *The Betrayal of the Negro*, 48-87.

for the Port of Beaufort was Smalls' reward for this support. Some Republican congressman, disappointed by Smalls' "late martyrdom in [the] Elliott contest" and impressed by his work for the party, petitioned President Harrison to appoint Smalls to the post, as did many citizens of Beaufort. Confident of success, Smalls wrote his son-in-law that Republican congressman would use "their influence to get any office for him."[3]

Smalls was not appointed collector without a fight, however. One of the other candidates for the post was a white Republican deputy customs collector, George Gage. "There are five Republicans (so called) who want to be the Collector of Customs for this district," Gage wrote to Francis N. Buck of Wilmington, Delaware, on March 6, 1889. One of them, Robert Smalls, "has no qualifications that fit him for the place, while he has several 'Points of Character,' that wholy [sic] unfit him for the place." It would be a "serious calamity" to make Smalls the collector, he continued, since the people of Beaufort had no confidence in him. If the collector were to be chosen by them Smalls had not "a ghost of a chance." Buck should use his position to help break down "the foreign Congressional influence in favor of Smalls." It was not a "Matter of Utmost importance" that he, Gage, should be the collector, but it was "such a Matter that Smalls should not be—he is ignorant, and politically as dishonest as any man I ever knew." Gage also indicated that his opposition to Smalls was based upon the ground that Smalls did "all in his power to help the democrats to carry this county [Elliott's victory] by Democratic methods, which Smalls is as loud as any Democrat in defending today." He discounted the claim of competence made by Senator Sherman in a letter to President Harrison in behalf of Smalls' candidacy. In another letter to his sister Mary, Gage argued that only "ignoramuses" in Beaufort had petitioned the President on Smalls' behalf and appealed to her to use her connections to "help us to defeat Smalls." In May Gage went to Washington to campaign for his candidacy but noticed that,

---

[3] All these letters are found in the Robert Smalls Custom File, National Archives, Washington, D.C.

though "the chances for Robert Smalls grew smaller every day," they might "still be large enough to give him the place."[4]

In addition to Gage, Thomas Miller, whom Smalls had supported in a futile congressional campaign in 1888, denounced Smalls on the grounds that he had cooperated with the Democrats to put up a fusion ticket in that election. Former political rival Whipper also charged that Robert Smalls, "but yesterday the idol of Republicans in this county," had gone into the "arms of the blood-stained Democracy that he has so long, so often, and so proudly denounced." To this alleged act of political treachery, Whipper added that Smalls had allowed a "disreputable gin mill" to operate in one of his buildings and that Smalls had not really abducted the *Planter*.[5]

Smalls answered all these charges in great detail. "I have never at any time or in any way sympathised with or assisted the Democratic Party," he wrote to President Harrison. On the contrary, he continued, he had always and would always oppose the Democrats in the belief that he was thereby "doing God service and my race a benefit." He charged that his opponents were "the lowest element in Southern politics," but conceded that an opposition so vocal might defeat him because a reputation was easier to tear down than to build up. The opponents, however,

> . . . cannot injure me with the people of the state who have known me through long years of trial as well as triumph, who have ever stood faithfully by me, and to whose cause I have never proved recreant in the past and whom I will never desert in their struggles for their rights, their ballots, and for the victory of the party which has done so much for the man they have suffered so much to serve.[6]

The allegations made by Smalls' opponents were unjustified and only reflected their desire for the collectorship. Before the

[4] George Gage to Francis N. Buck, March 6, 1889; Gage to Townsend, March 4, 1889; Gage to Thomas Miller, April 17, 1889; Gage to Mary, March 5, 1889; Gage to Messrs. Geo. McQuesten & Co., May 9, 1889; The Papers of George Gage, Duke University, Durham, N.C.

[5] W. J. Whipper, pamphlet; Thomas Miller to William Windom, April 22, 1889; all these in the Robert Smalls Custom File, National Archives, Washington, D.C.

[6] Robert Smalls to Benjamin Harrison, May 7, 1889, Custom File, National Archives.

contest, George Gage had confided to a friend that, though Smalls' political sun was setting, "there was a great deal of good about him." Shortly after Smalls' appointment was confirmed, Gage also asked Smalls to endorse his application for the position of Deputy Collector of Internal Revenue for the district. He had earlier tried to get Smalls to support him for Special Deputy to the customs collector for Beaufort. Smalls' appointment had been announced on June 13, 1889, and confirmed by January 25, 1890. The salary was $1000 per annum, plus commission fees of 3 per cent, the total not to exceed $3000 per annum. Except for the period from February 15, 1894 to June 22, 1898, Smalls held the position until June 1913.[7]

Though scanty and generally inadequate, the available data indicate that Smalls performed creditably as the customs collector for Beaufort. From his two-room office and with a staff which varied from six to seven, he directed the daily routine of the new position with thoroughness. All merchant vessels arriving from a foreign country or coastwise were regularly entered before permission was granted either to discharge or take on cargo. Cargo shipped from Beaufort included wood, phosphate, and cotton. A weekly report of cotton shipments and a statement of public funds were made to the Treasury Department. At the end of each month reports on the entrance and clearance of all vessels engaged in foreign trade, statements of receipts and disbursements, records of marine documents issued, and the value of imports and exports were meticulously compiled, and were eventually incorporated into a final annual report for each fiscal year. Business, though it did not prosper, was certainly on the increase at the port. In 1890 it cost about $1.01 to collect $1 at Beaufort. At the turn of the century, it was estimated that it cost $0.719 to collect $1, an excellent figure compared with those for other ports like New York where it cost about $2 to collect $1.[8] Besides,

[7] George Gage to Robert Smalls, August 12, 1889; Gage to Eugene Webster, August 12, 1889; Gage to J. D. Taylor, November 10, 1888; Records, Bureau of Customs, Treasury Department, Washington, D.C.; C. A. Freeman to Dorothy Sterling, June 19, 1956.

[8] The Reports of Beaufort can be found in the Annual Report of the Secretary of the Treasury for the years 1890 to 1913. That of 1890, for ex-

periodic examinations by a board of appraisers revealed no in-
accuracies in the records kept by Smalls and his staff, nor was
the port one of those frequently listed as destitute of business
in these years.[9]

The regularity with which Smalls was reappointed and confirmed, often without challenge, is further evidence that he ran
his office well. In 1906, Smalls went to Washington to present
his petition for reappointment but was met at the station by a
close friend with the news that his reappointment had already
been confirmed. In 1910, some leading Democrats in Beaufort
also joined in a petition, "regardless of party," recommending
Smalls' reappointment. Similar petitions were filed in behalf of
Smalls' candidacy in 1912, when the opposition of the Democratic
senators from his state, hitherto ineffective, prevented his reappointment. "There is no democrat of any prominence in this
place who have [sic] not signed the petition," Smalls wrote a
friend. Prominent Republicans also joined in the fight to secure
the appointment for Smalls. Senator Knute Nelson, Chairman of
the Committee on Commerce, promised to help Smalls get the
job. "I remember you very well from my service with you in the
House and I am familiar with your record and entirely friendly
to you and your cause," he whote to Smalls. Senator William
Alden Smith, Chairman of the Committee on Territories also
promised to help because he felt Smalls was "in every way deserving of the honor which you wear so worthily." Other promises of support came from Senators Boies Penrose, Chairman,
Committee on Finance; George C. Perkins, Chairman, Committee on Naval Affairs; Theodore Burton, Chairman, Committee
on Expenditures in the Treasury Department; and Senator
Robert La Follette. One Senator pledged support because "I

---

ample, listed 69 foreign vessels, 64 coastwise as entering Beaufort. The port
cleared 100 foreign and 33 coastwise vessels. In 1893, 31 foreign and 26 coastwise vessels entered, and 54 foreign and 4 coastwise vessels were cleared from
the port. Annual Report of the Secretary of the Treasury, 1890 (Washington,
D.C., 1891), 783; also Annual Report, 1893, 785.

9 From the 1880's to 1913, each succeeding Secretary of the Treasury recommended the abolition of customs posts at several ports which were rendered
unnecessary by changing transportation needs.

remember as a boy reading of your services to the Union cause."[10]
All these failed to get Smalls reappointed because of the opposition of the senators from his state. Accepting defeat, Smalls wrote
Knute Nelson that he had been holding office by appointment
of the President for quite a while and had always had the opposition of the senators from his state. He did not expect their
support now nor in the future, "being myself what I have always
been and expect to continue, a straightout republican." His only
concern was that "in a senate with a republican majority under
a republican administration, the democratic senators can defeat
the confirmation of a republican."[11]

Smalls also used his connections with prominent Republicans
to get offices for his family and friends, among them Dr. William
D. Crum, whom Smalls looked upon as a son and a protégé. A
pioneer black physician, Crum had graduated from Harvard in
1880 and was considered to be "one of the best citizens of
Charleston, an admirable man in every way." In 1903, through
letters, personal appearances, and the influences of his friends,
Smalls was able to get Crum appointed and confirmed as the
collector of customs for Charleston, despite the opposition of the
Tillmanites. He himself would not take a foreign post in Liberia
or Haiti, because, according to his son, these were "appointments
set up as Negro office," but actively encouraged Crum to do so.[12]
In 1910 he won Republican support for Crum's appointment as
Minister to Liberia. "No one who was not in line and pledged
to stand by the Republicans of the State," Smalls confided to a
friend, could have Federal office in South Carolina.[13]

[10] Smalls to Whitfield McKinlay, August 19, 1910; Smalls to McKinlay,
May 11, 1912; McKinlay to Smalls, May 20, 1912; Nelson to Smalls, May 30,
1913; W. A. Smith to Smalls, June 16, 1912; Theodore Burton to Smalls, July
12, 1913, Woodson Papers.

[11] Knute Nelson to Smalls, August 20, 1912; Smalls to Nelson, August 22,
1912, Woodson Papers.

[12] Smalls to McKinlay, January 10, 1903; January 26, 1903, Woodson Papers.
This reason was given by William Smalls who also indicated that his father
would have taken a South American post, preferably Venezuela, if offered.
Also Simkins, *Pitchfork Ben Tillman*, 416-418. See also Willard B. Gatewood,
"William D. Crum: A Negro in Politics," *Journal of Negro History*, LVII
(October 1968), 307-320.

[13] Smalls to McKinlay, October 22, 1902, Woodson Papers.

To continue enjoying these favors, Smalls had to keep his
county secure for the Republican party. Since Beaufort was a
Republican enclave in a Democratic state, this called for organi-
zational ability. Apart from using the spoils of office to keep
supporters in line, Smalls organized the blacks in his district to
deliver whatever votes they still had to the Republican party.
In 1903, because of an impending municipal election, Smalls
turned down an invitation from McKinlay to come to Washington. "We have never lost an election here since reconstruction," he wrote a friend. There was "some talk of a democratic
candidate being sprung on us at the last moment," he continued,
adding that he wanted to remain at Beaufort to look after things.[14]

On the national scene, Smalls interpreted opposition to the
Republican party as a great threat to black interest. He remained
steadfast in his belief that only Republicans could save the
blacks. To his friends Whitfield McKinlay, who was trying to
influence President Taft to change his Southern policies, Smalls
sent hearty congratulations because "you are still alert for those
things that will be for the good of the Race." Though disenchanted by Taft's Southern policy, which encouraged the suppression of blacks in the South, and though warned that many
blacks in the North would vote the Progressive ticket in the
election of 1912, Smalls looked unfavorably on Theodore Roosevelt's candidacy. "No one had a higher regard for Theo. Roosevelt
than I," Smalls wrote to a friend. "But his course in trying to
split the party of Lincoln and Grant and other illustrious men,
that party which unshakled [sic] the necks of four millions human
beings, and by whose acts might elect a democratic president . . .
I have lost all the respect for such a man." Roosevelt's position
might result in the election of Woodrow Wilson, who, a Southerner by birth, would be "under the entire domination of the
South, where more than ⅔ of the Negro voters had been robbed
of their franchise." Such men as the governor of South Carolina,
who had "refused to commission a single Negro as even a notary
public in the state," would be Wilson's advisers. He appealed
to every black man in the North to vote solidly for the Repub-

14 Smalls to McKinlay, January 10, 1903, Woodson Papers.

lican candidate, President Taft. Now that the convention had acted, he concluded, it behooved all black leaders to work for the election of Taft. For him there would be "No new or Progressive party. With me the Grand Old Party of Lincoln is above all other considerations." Despite its liberal and progressive achievement in several areas, Wilson's policies on race justified many of Smalls' fears. Even the black bishop, Alexander Walters, who campaigned actively for Wilson and had been offered the post of Minister to Liberia in 1915, voiced, in 1917, his keen disappointment in Wilson. With the institutionalization and expansion of segregation in Federal department buildings in Washington, a policy which Taft had begun, the Wilson Administration in fact left blacks in no doubt that the President's "New Freedom" was to be "all for the white man and little for the Negro." By the time of the outbreak of the First World War, several black leaders voiced the opinion that all they were expecting from the Wilson's administration was "nigger sections in all the Washington departments."[15]

Though no longer their official representative, Smalls continued to work for his people through his political contacts. In 1901, the congressional Committee on Banking and Currency was considering a bill to close up the Freedman's Savings and Trust Company and convert all its assets, after June 13, 1902, into cash to be turned over to the trustees of Howard University for the benefit of that institution. Smalls sought to influence the Committee not to transfer all the assets to Howard. A branch of the bank had been established in Beaufort in 1864, he argued in an open letter, and depositors had lost between $75,000 and $100,000 when the bank was closed in 1874 and Congress refused to pay the losses incurred by the depositors. Since Beaufort citizens would derive no direct benefit from Howard, it would be an injustice to the descendants of Beaufort depositors if all the assets were turned over to Howard. A portion of the assets should be allocated to the Beaufort free school for black children founded in 1867. "We have endeavored to keep the property in as good

15 Smalls to McKinlay, November 10, 1909 and September 12, 1912; McKinlay to Smalls, June 12, 1912, Woodson Papers; also *Crisis*, V (November 1912), 29.

condition as we could without any aid from any source," Smalls pleaded. Part of the assets of the Freedman's Savings and Trust Company would help improve conditions in this school, which was serving about four hundred pupils. Smalls' plea was rejected.[16]

Robert Smalls remained unshaken in his belief that given equal opportunity, the black man would perform as well as any white in any capacity. "Tell all and any of those men who says [sic] colored men cannot do the work or understand the laws of the Customs, that they simply don't know what they are talking about," he wrote when describing the performance of Julius I. Washington, his special deputy as customs collector. Washington had just been in office two months, he continued, yet "he had run it in my absence with perfect satisfaction. All the negro wants is equal opportunities." On another occasion he rejected the suggestion that those blacks who performed well in all fields of endeavor were of a special breed. "In your letter before the last," he wrote to McKinlay, "you stated that you thought yourself that all Negroes in office, except myself, are more than apt to be dropped." He continued:

> Now my dear friend, I am a Negro and nothing could make me otherwise, and when the time comes, I have no doubt that I will still be a Negro. Any little thing that a white man does makes him a big man, but no matter what a Negro does he is still nothing. He, in the white man's estimation, can do nothing that will make him a great man.[17]

He believed that the prejudice against the black was because the black man was "improving, for in every instance where he is put alongside the white man in a test of any kind, he either comes out ahead or stands his equal. . . . This is the reason why every white man, especially in the South, seems now willing to see him relegated to the rear before he becomes too powerful and strong." He did not despair, however, because "not with-

---

[16] Robert Smalls to Member, Committee on Banking and Currency, House of Representatives, Washington, D.C., February 19, 1901, Newspaper Clippings by Mrs. Hall in Miscellaneous Newspaper Clippings, Moorland Foundation, Howard University.

[17] Smalls to McKinlay, October 22, 1902; Smalls to McKinlay, November 10, 1909, Woodson Papers.

standing all this, the same God still lives in whom we place our hope."

Robert Smalls' preoccupation with public affairs did not imply neglect of his family responsibilities. From his first marriage with Hannah Jones, Smalls had three children, Elizabeth, Robert Jr., and Sara. Hannah died in 1883, and in 1895 Smalls married Annie Wigg, a graduate of Avery School, Charleston, and a teacher, from whom he had a son, William Robert. Robert Jr. died in childhood. In his leisure hours, Smalls took the children fishing or riding around the Islands. "He was an affectionate and loving father, who wanted his children to have whatever he did not have," one granddaughter recalls. A strong believer in education, Smalls wanted his children to have the best he could afford. Sara was educated at Mine Normal School in Washington, D.C., and at the Boston Conservatory of Music. She taught music for some years at the South Carolina Teachers College at Orangeburg. Elizabeth was educated at Allen's English and Classical School in West Newton, Massachusetts. She served as her father's secretary when he was in Congress and married Samuel J. Bamfield, former editor of the Beaufort *Free South*. When her husband died, she became the postmistress for Beaufort and later served as secretary at the Penn School at Frogmore. William Robert Smalls was educated at the Armstrong Manual Training High School in Washington, D.C., and at the University of Pittsburgh. After a brief teaching career in Texas, Virginia, and Kentucky, he served in the First World War, and now lives at Toledo, Ohio, where he works with the Urban League.

Despite high spirits in the last years of his life, Smalls' health was gradually giving way. In 1906, after a brief trip to Massachusetts where he addressed the commencement meeting of Phi Beta Kappa of Harvard University, Smalls was taken ill with peritonitis. Though operated upon and sent to Freedmen's Hospital in Washington, he never quite recovered. The operation never healed properly and Smalls walked with a slight limp. "My friend I am not well at all," he wrote to McKinlay in 1912, "my limbs bother me from my knees to my feet, from numbness, but I am able to get about just the same." He could not attend the Republican convention in 1912 because he could not "very well have endured the fatigue and the harrowing scenes." Heretofore a regular visitor to Washington and the North, Smalls for the most part stuck close to home after 1912. His letters of these years bear the marks of physical and mental deterioration. Even his sense of humor gave way and he became, according to his son, "a cantankerous old man." After June 1914, he was mostly confined to his bed. On February 22, 1915, the old hero passed away, leaving behind three children, several grandchildren, and a considerable amount of property.[18]

On February 26, 1915, the citizens of Beaufort and many prominent blacks gathered in the First Avenue Baptist Church where Smalls himself had worshiped for more than ten years. This time they had not come to listen to Smalls' "fine story" about the *Planter* or his political campaigns, or to honor him with cheers and pledges of support. Now they could honor him only with their tears. The Allen's Brass Band which had always accompanied him on political campaigns was there, but this time it played the solemn funeral march. Dr. Bythe Wood, a Beaufort minister, reminded the weeping crowd that they were there to pay the last respects to "a great citizen." Reverend P. P. Watson of Orangeburg added that the deceased was "one of the greatest Negroes." Dr. Coit, presiding elder of the African Methodist Episcopal Church for Beaufort, catalogued the "many beneficial legislative enactments attributed to the fertile brain of the general." After an impressive service and a Masonic ceremony, Robert Smalls was buried in the A.M.E. Churchyard on Craven Street. Very appropriately, the choir sang "Shall we meet beyond the river!" The funeral was "the largest ever held in this city and the floral offerings were numerous and beautiful," commented the Savannah *Tribune* on this last respect paid to a great black man and an authentic American hero.[19]

The Civil War and Reconstruction decades provided black people with a perplexing introduction into politics. Generally

[18] Smalls to McKinlay, May 22, 1912, Woodson Papers; Woodson, "Robert Smalls and His Descendants," 30-33.
[19] Savannah *Tribune*, March 6, 1915; see also *Crisis* (April 1915); New York *Age*, March 4, 1915.

speaking, most of those who assumed political responsibilities were unprepared for the enormous challenges involved in their newly acquired status. Even those who—either by self purchase, fleeing, or the actions of some masters—had become free before the Civil War were no better off than their recently emancipated brothers in this regard. In either situation black people had been denied political experiences, a prerequisite for the formation and running of an intelligent government. Suddenly granted great opportunities and responsibilities, they had to find their way through baffling problems, often irresistible temptations, and the frequently bad examples of their white mentors.

The black leaders in South Carolina in these years were a mixed lot. Among them were highly trained college graduates like the scrupulously honest but somewhat moderate Cardozo and the handsome black lawyer, Robert Brown Elliott; barely literate people like Joseph Hayne Rainey who went from his barber's chair to represent Georgetown at the 1868 convention, the state senate, and the United States Congress, Alonzo Jacob Ransier who had worked as a shipping clerk before the war and served variously as the chairman of the state Republican executive committee and lieutenant governor before going to Congress in 1873, and Robert Smalls; and those like Beverly Nash who went from the plantation to the perches of power and could neither read nor write when Reconstruction began. Given their differing backgrounds and experiences, their political performances were bound to vary. Some of them became brilliant politicians while some never understood what political power meant. Some, with brilliant ideas and impeccable qualifications failed while others, perhaps less brilliant, excelled at political in-fighting and were effective on the stump. The black leaders were not a homogeneous group to whom such characteristics as corruption, laziness, dishonesty, ignorance, incapability, incompetence, and vindictiveness can be assigned. They were neither all good men nor all bad.[20]

[20] For a good treatment of these stereotypes, see W. E. B. Du Bois, "The Propaganda of History," in *Black Reconstruction,* 711-728. Lerone Bennett, Jr. discusses the performance of South Carolina Reconstruction leaders in *Black Power U.S.A.* (Baltimore, 1967), 155-167.

"One of the surprising results of the Reconstruction Period," the Negro educator Booker T. Washington wrote, "was that there should spring from among the members of a race that had been held so long in slavery, so large a number of shrewd, resolute, resourceful, and even brilliant men, who became, during this brief period of storms and stress, the political leaders of the newly enfranchised race."[21] Robert Smalls fits well into this description. Daring, cool-headed, keen of mind, courageous, and firm on the principle of the equality of all men without regard to race and color, Robert Smalls was an outstanding leader of the Reconstruction decades and after.

Throughout his politically active years, Robert Smalls thought of himself not only as representing black people but as being black himself. He was not ashamed of his race and never lost an opportunity to remind whites of this fact. He was emphatic on the point that he was only one among his fellow blacks and insisted that his colleagues, black and white, see him as such. Smalls understood that blacks were discriminated against as a people and that the individual black person who did achieve "exceptional" status was really no freer from discrimination.

Except for the brief period in 1862, when the *Planter* episode brought him into national prominence, Robert Smalls never won the national plaudits showered on either Booker T. Washington or W. E. B. Du Bois. Though he maintained constant contact with Republican national administrations during his politically active years and profited from the spoils of office, thus functioning partly as an "out-group based leader," Smalls was essentially an "ethnic" leader with firm roots in his community. In a community that had no clearly defined upper or political class, Smalls, together with a few other individuals, came to symbolize the aspirations of the Beaufort blacks. He affected the patterns of behavior of his constituents, and wielded enormous power within his community, mainly because of his leadership qualities and because he delivered something more tangible than the rhetoric of racial unity and hope of improvement in terms of the educa-

21 Booker T. Washington, *The Story of the Negro* (2 vols., New York, 1909), II, 22-23.

tional and economic projects he promoted. If successful leadership can be judged by an ability to instill among the following a certain high degree of morale and an effectiveness in securing community goals, Smalls was certainly an effective leader of the Beaufort blacks in these years.

Unlike many of his Southern contemporaries, including Booker T. Washington, Smalls did not, publicly or privately, show any respect for the system of race prejudice, and did not regard political or civil rights as a luxury, but as fundamental to the acquisition of the other needs of black people. He realized that political power was necessary for any economic gains, as is illustrated by his constant effort to use his political connections to secure economic benefits for his community. "The battle of life" for which Robert Smalls asked that black people be given "an equal chance" was an economic as well as a political one.

Since he accepted the political system of his day as a viable vehicle for effecting change and thereby eliminating the discrimination to which blacks were subjected, Smalls' political stance was essentially one of protest as opposed to any sort of revolution. To protest within the system meant that Smalls, as well as many of his black contemporaries, had to appeal to white sympathy, sense of decency, and fairness. The theme of fairness or equal treatment runs through nearly all of Smalls' important speeches. When making appeals in behalf of black people, Smalls always called for a return to the ideals on which the nation was founded.

Like many of his contemporaries, Smalls saw integration as the goal of the black struggle and believed that the "inherent justice" of the American system of government as expressed in the Declaration of Independence would triumph over the forces that had conspired to make the country depart from its principles. Black people, in his thinking, because they possessed in abundance those "virtues which adorn the human race"—gentleness, patience, affection, and generosity—would play an important part in making the American dream come true. He firmly believed and constantly quoted the words of President Lincoln to the effect that "the ballot in the hands of the black man may serve in some trying hour to come to preserve the jewel of liberty

to the diadem of the Republic." As for white people, he per-
ceived the significance of Reconstruction policy as a white commitment to the goal of equality for all Americans, irrespective
of their color. Using the advantage of hindsight, we know that
Smalls' hope for integration, equal opportunity, and practical
citizenship for black people proved unrealistic. Reality was the
emergence of a color-caste system imbedded in the laws, behavior,
and attitudes of white America. Even as he lay dying, segregation
which he had fought bitterly against in Congress was becoming
a "way of life" in the nation's capital, and timely death saved
Smalls from the worst that was to come. Perhaps he might still
have remained hopeful if he had been spared. But sooner or
later, he would have found, as we have today, that he was merely
dreaming and that dreams, however inspiring, are not nutritive.
More than half a century after his death, the extent of white
commitment to equal citizenship and opportunity for their black
countrymen remains doubtful.

A NOTE ON BIBLIOGRAPHY

IT HAS BEEN no easy task to put together this story of Robert Smalls. A black slave for the first twenty-three years of his life who was denied the benefit of any education, and a man concerned mostly with political issues vital to his own and his people's survival for much of his adult life, Smalls did not put his thoughts on paper for the use of a later generation. In this situation, the historian is forced to depend excessively on public records which unfortunately do not always reveal the inner workings of a man's mind. Moreover, most of the newspapers which have been used extensively in this study appeared at a time when Negrophobia was an accepted editorial habit. The writer, however, has felt that the life of Robert Smalls is such a valuable commentary on the hopes, fears, aspirations, triumphs, and tragedies of Black Reconstruction leaders that he has undertaken to reconstruct a story which draws from a variety of sources, including written and oral evidence.

Among the manuscript sources for the study, the letters of Robert Smalls found in the Carter G. Woodson Papers in the Manuscript Division of the Library of Congress, and the Robert Smalls Custom File in the National Archives, were very valuable. Unfortunately, both collections contain letters written in the last twenty-five years of Smalls' life. For Smalls' activities in the Union

Navy during the war, the Records of Smalls and the *Planter* in the National Archives is a useful source. The Diary of William F. Allen, 1863-1864, at the Wisconsin State Historical Society Library in Madison, the Papers of Solomon Portland Chase in the Library of Congress, Notes and Extracts from Letters Written from Beaufort, 1862-1863, by Kate Foote and Harriet Foote Hawley at the Beaufort Township Library, the William Channing Gannet Papers at the University of Rochester, the Edwin Stanton Papers at the Library of Congress, and the Port Royal Correspondence at the National Archives, all contain valuable information on the Port Royal Experiment in which Smalls played a prominent part. The Papers of Daniel Chamberlain and Wade Hampton together with Legislative System, 1866-1877, Election Miscellaneous, Beaufort County, all in the South Carolina Archives at Columbia, South Carolina, contain material dealing with the years Smalls was a prominent state politician. The papers of W. J. Whipper at the Moorland Foundation's Library at Howard University contain data for the political disagreement among Sea Island Republicans in the 1880's and 1890's. The Moorland Foundation Library also has an Address given by Thomas Miller on February 10, 1930, in which he paid tribute to Robert Smalls, and a typescript by Henry Bowen Anthony titled Integrity of Republican Administration which deals with South Carolina. The Schomburg Collection in New York has a typescript in which William Robert Smalls discusses the life of his father, as well as a pamphlet by Sarah Smalls containing the speeches made by her father at the Constitutional Convention of 1895. The Papers of George Gage at Duke University, Durham, North Carolina, contains letters dealing with the controversy over the appointment of Smalls as a customs collector. Extremely valuable was the collection of Smalls materials made by Mrs. Dorothy Sterling of Rye, New York, which, among other things, contains letters to and from her to descendants of Henry McKee, interviews with William Smalls and others who knew Robert Smalls personally and were still alive in 1955 when Mrs. Sterling researched at Beaufort, and numerous newspaper clippings. This writer also interviewed several people at Beaufort, including Mrs. Wright, the principal of the Robert Smalls Junior

High, and Mrs. Helen Christensen who has a vivid recollection of Reconstruction days in Beaufort.

In addition to the above, I have depended heavily on newspapers published in Beaufort, Charleston, and other areas in the state and nation which concerned themselves with events in South Carolina generally and in the Sea Islands particularly. Beaufort papers, especially the *Free South, New South, Republican* and *Tribune,* were very full, though often conflicting, in their coverage of political campaigns and other issues in which Smalls played a prominent part. These papers are available only at the Beaufort Township Library. The Charleston *News and Courier* (*Daily Courier* before 1867) the most influential newspaper in South Carolina at this time, was used rather extensively but very carefully as were the Charleston *Sun* and *World.* The Columbia *Daily Register, Guardian, State* and *Union Herald* were also consulted. Among out-of-state papers consulted were *Harper's Weekly, The Liberator, The Nation, The National Anti-Slavery Standard, National Freedmen, National Republican,* New Orleans *Tribune,* New York *Evening Post,* New York *Journal of Commerce, The New York Times,* New York *Tribune, Philadelphia Inquirer,* Philadelphia *Press,* Pittsburg *Gazette, Providence Journal,* Savannah *Tribune,* and *Weekly Anglo-American.*

Published documents were very extensively used in the study. *The Acts and Resolutions of the General Assembly of the State of South Carolina, Journal of the House of Representatives of the State of South Carolina, Reports and Resolutions of the General Assembly of the State of South Carolina,* were consulted for the years Smalls served in the state legislature. Unfortunately, very few of the discussions over some vital questions introduced in the legislature are fully entered. For the years Smalls was in the United States Congress, the *Congressional Record* together with the *House Report* and *Documents* were used. The *Official Records of the Union and Confederate Armies* contain useful information on Small's abduction and subsequent handling of the *Planter.* Other published documents used in various parts of the study include *Official Proceedings of Republican National Conventions* (1872-1880) (Washington, D.C., 1908), and the *Report of the Committee Appointed for the Purpose of Securing to the Colored People the Right to Use the Street Cars* (Philadelphia, 1867).

Contemporary events in the state were often discussed in many diaries and travellers' accounts. Most useful in this category is *The Journal of Charlotte L. Foten* edited by Ray Allen Billington. It should be noted, however, that the references by Forten to a Robert Smalls (page 155) which Billington takes as the Robert Smalls of this study is incorrect. At no time did Smalls keep a store in Beaufort. Elizabeth Pearson's *Letters from Port Royal* (Boston, 1906), Benjamin Perry's *Reminiscences of Public Men with Speeches and Addresses* (Greenville, S.C., 1889), A. E. Stephens' *Enfranchisement and Citizenship: Addresses and Papers of E. L. Pearson* (Boston, 1896), Edward King's *The Southern States of North America* (Glasgow, 1875), and George Campbell's *White and Black: The Outcome of a Visit to the United States* (London, 1879) contain valuable references to Smalls or to issues in which he was involved. James S. Pike's *The Prostrate State: South Carolina Under Negro Government,* recently republished by the Louisiana State University Press, is best seen as the fulminations of a disappointed and disgruntled liberal with no sympathy for the problems the black politicians faced. A graphic description of the flag-raising ceremony in 1864 is presented in J. C. French and Edward Gary, *The Trip of the Steamer Oceanus to Fort Sumter, April 14, 1865* (Brooklyn, 1865).

There has been only one full-length biography of Robert Smalls, Dorothy Sterling's thoroughly researched and fascinating *Captain of the Planter: The Story of Robert Smalls* (New York, 1958) for young readers. Smalls' escape with the *Planter* has been the subject of some articles, among these Benjamin Quarles' "Abduction of the 'Planter,'" *Civil War History,* IV (March 1958); M. Rosbow, "The Abduction of the Planter," *Crisis* (April 1949). *A Short Sketch of the Military and Political Career and Public Services of General Robert Smalls* (Washington, D.C., 1882), a typescript at the Wisconsin State Historical Society, is interesting but largely uncritical, as are entries on Robert Smalls in Russel Adams' *Great Heroes Past and Present* (Chicago 1963) and in William H. Quick's *Negro Stars in All Ages of the World* (Richmond, Va., 1898). Other accounts of Smalls' career are

Charles Cowley, *The Romance of History in the Black Country and the Romance of War in the Career of General Robert Smalls* (Lowell, Mass., 1882) whose title indicates the nature of the content, W. J. Simmons, *Men of the Mark* (Ohio, 1887), Carter C. Woodson, "Robert Smalls and His Descendants," *Negro History Bulletin* (November 1947), Benjamin Brawley, *Negro Builders and Heroes* (Chapel Hill, N.C., 1937), William W. Brown, *The Black Man: His Antecedents, His Genius, and His Achievements* (Boston, 1863), John Bruce, *Smalls Robert: A Case in Point* (Washington, D.C., 1888), Francis B. Simkins, "Robert Smalls" in *Dictionary of American Biography*, 17, 224 (New York, 1935), and "The Late Ex-Congressman Robert Smalls," *Crisis* (April 1915). Smalls' appeals in behalf of the Sea Islanders while he was in Philadelphia in 1864 is discussed in "Captain Robert Smalls Addresses the General Conference of 1864," *A.M.E. Church Review* (January-March 1955). Robert Smalls himself discussed the political situation in his state in his only publication, "Election Methods in South Carolina," *North Atlantic Review*, CLI (November 1890). Deborah Moore's Master of Arts essay at Columbia University, 1968, "The King of Beaufort," is a generally well-written work but is rather brief on Smalls' activities as a state legislator.

Several studies dealing with Reconstruction in the South in general and in South Carolina in particular were consulted and these are listed in the bibliographical section of my original monograph, "From Servitude to Service: Robert Smalls, 1839-1915," at the University of Wisconsin Library in Madison. Some of these are also cited in the relevant sections of the footnotes. The following, however, were rather extensively used and merit particular mention. Willie Lee Rose, *Rehearsal for Reconstruction: The Port Royal Experiment* (New York, 1964) is an excellent study of its subject. W. E. B. Du Bois, *Black Reconstruction in America,* reprinted in paperback by Meridian recently, is still the best analysis of that neglected but extremely important subject. It should be supplemented with Lerone Bennett, Jr., *Black Power U.S.A.: The Human Side of Reconstruction* (Penguin, 1967), fascinating but poorly researched, and Robert Cruden's recently published *The Negro in Reconstruction* (Prentice Hall,

1969) which does a good job at pulling together ideas expressed by others in various studies. George Brown Tindall's *South Carolina Negroes, 1877-1900* and Joel Williamson's *After Slavery: The Negro in South Carolina During Reconstruction,* taken together, give an accurate idea of the political, economic, and social problems that the South Carolina blacks faced in the Reconstruction years. *Reconstruction: An Anthology of Revisionist Writings* by Kenneth Stampp and Leon Litwack (Louisiana State University, Baton Rouge, 1969), is a welcome addition to the growing body of literature dealing with the critical years between the Civil War and the First World War, during which black people played a conspicuous, if not prominent, part in the political life of the nation.

INDEX